TIMOTHY A. LOWELL

IS IT GONNA BLOW UP?

Creating Happy Young Scientists,
Engineers, Builders and Artists

Active Art & Science

http://www.activeartandscience.com

Active Art & Science Press
524 26th Ave South
Seattle, WA 98144
Activeartandscience.com

ISBN: 978-1-54393-082-5

First Edition
Printed in the United States of America

Library of Congress Cataloging-in-Publication Data
Names: Lowell, Timothy A.
Title: Is it Gonna Blow Up?: Creating happy young scientists, engineers, builders and artists/Timothy A. Lowell
Description: First Edition / Seattle, Washington / Active Art & Science Press / (2018)
Subjects: Science – Miscellanea – Juvenile Literature. / Science – experiments – Juvenile literature

Dedication:

To my wife Mary: without your love and
support, this book would not exist!

Table of Contents

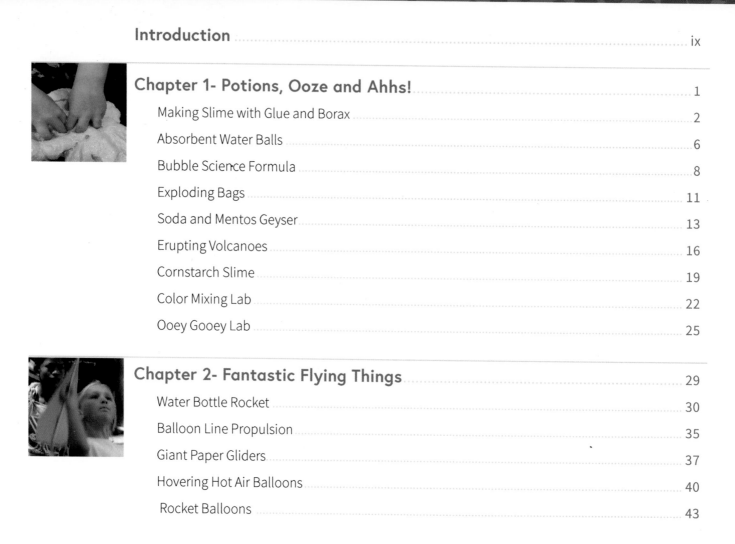

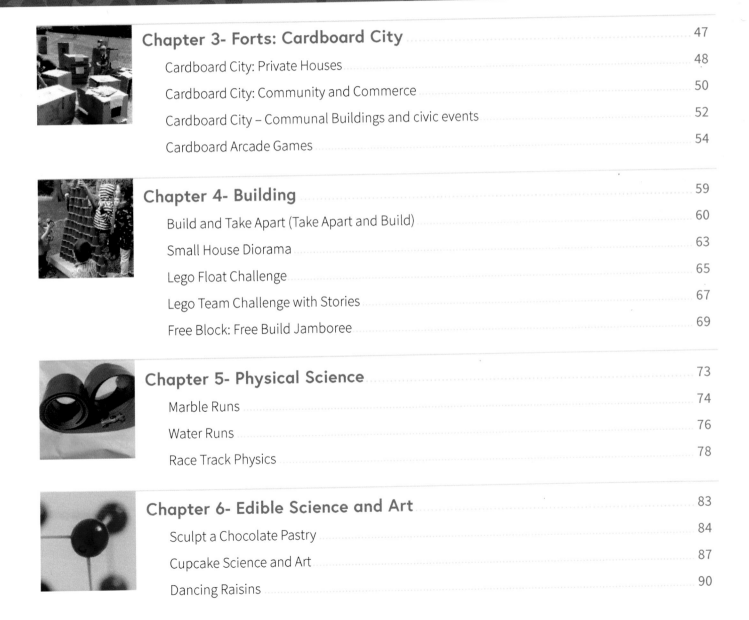

Introduction

The student was in tears, looking at her materials, unable to begin. She told me, "I can't do it." When I asked her why, she answered, "I'm no good at art." As we talked, it seemed to me that the pain of her belief was as fresh to her now as it had been 80 years earlier. This experience at a Silver Lake, WA senior center and others like it pushed me to develop lesson plans that would turn learning into a positive experience for everyone.

My first goal in writing this book is for readers to use the activities and lessons chapters as a guide to introduce subjects in a positive way and bring hands-on, confidence-building experiments to children. My second goal is fun. My own education in how to avoid boredom and maximize fun began when I was a single parent and childcare was difficult to find. I often brought my youngest daughter with me to class, and she insisted on bringing her best friend with her. I would set them up in the back of the room while I conducted the lesson. The two girls would participate in the project and on the drive home rigorously critique my teaching. My daughter would say, "Dad, it was so boring when you did…." Her friend would follow by saying, "Yes, that was boring; some of the grown-ups liked it but the kids hated it." They were brutally candid. From that time on, I have applied their example to every lesson and solicited critique from students during and after the activity. Each lesson in this book has been honed by multiple children's *thumbs up, thumbs down* honesty.

Each activity recipe includes materials, how to do it with a large group, the lesson behind it, a preschool version and vocabulary. Most of the materials you will use can be purchased easily and inexpensively at grocery and hardware stores. Every activity was developed with budget efficiency in mind. The concepts covered in most activities are tied to Pre-K-5 learning standards.

One of my favorite parts of each section is the preschool science version. Bringing science to preschool children is a profound experience. Children aged 3-5 respond to activities with awe, joy and delight; they absorb experiences like sponges. The children are developing so rapidly that their response to a project changes each time you present it, so repetition is a plus. In fact, I have found that repeating projects is beneficial to all children's learning. Concepts that don't stick the first time become clear on the second or third try. Every time I hear the "we want slime" chant from my students, I remember that with repetition comes mastery. Before you know it, your students will be enthusiastically looking forward to science time, telling you that they are good at science!

Introducing subjects as "play" is an effective and developmentally appropriate way to foster lifelong appreciation and confidence in learning. My hope is that students come away from an activity feeling that they like the subject, they are capable of it and they are good at it. Early childhood interest and confidence leads to success and fulfillment in later years.

Use the activity recipes in this book to create an enrichment program, supplement your existing program or just have fun with science, technology, engineering, art and math. When you add the exercise (11 group games), you have all the ingredients needed to enjoy a nurturing, developmental enrichment program.

I hope you and your children have as much fun as I do.

Tim Lowell
Seattle, WA
2018

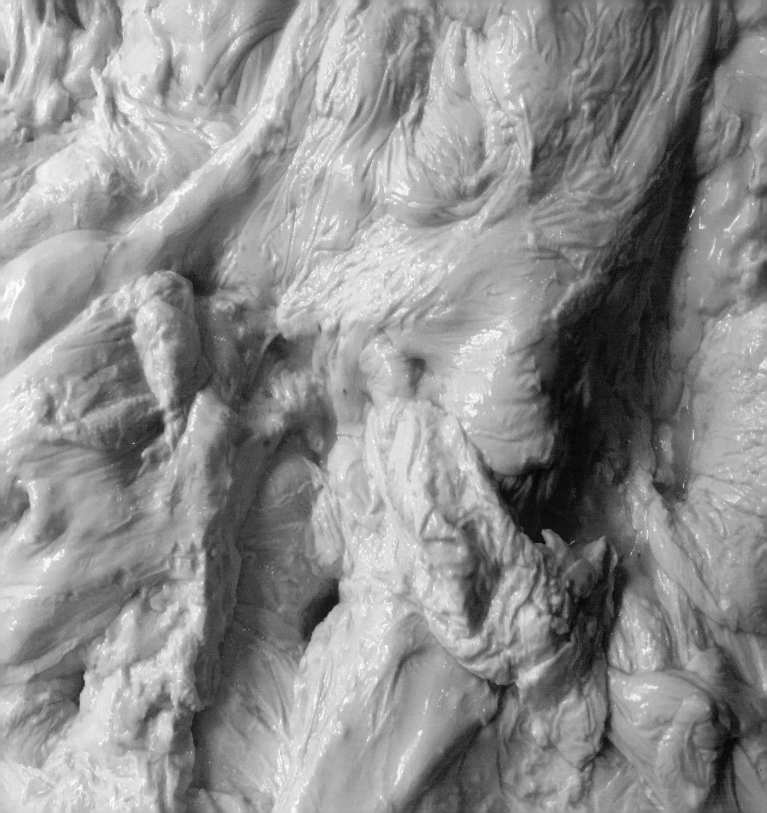

CHAPTER 1

POTIONS, OOZE AND AHHS!

Making Slime with Glue and Borax

The Aha! moment of making slime is seeing instant chemical change that turns your glue mix into a completely different rubbery substance. You will have great fun playing with your finished slime: shaping, spinning, blowing, pinching and stamping it into different shapes.

Mixing glue, borax laundry detergent and color creates an instant example of chemical change and is a fun toy to play with. Use slime as a make and take-home experiment or combine individual slimes to create a large tactile blob as part of your classroom science curiosities.

Materials:

- One 16-ounce plastic cup or small plastic bowl
- One wood popsicle stick
- Food coloring or water-based colorant; make sure you have red, blue and yellow
- 2 to 4 ounces of white glue (Elmer's Glue-All is best)
- 2 to 4 ounces of water
- A half teaspoon of borax detergent powder (1 teaspoon borax per 8 ounces of water)

These amounts are per person. Use 2-quart water pitchers for the water and borax mixture. Add 1.5- 2 tablespoons borax for each quart of water. Try to limit the food coloring to no more than 12-15 drops per student; 4 drops per color when they are mixing colors.

How to:

1. Pour the glue into cups or bowls

2. Add drops of food coloring to the glue and mix with the popsicle stick.

3. Mix borax and water and add it to the glue (equal amounts glue to borax/water mix).

4. Stir with the stick first and then use hands to be sure that every part of the glue touches the borax/water solution to cure it.

5. The slime is fully cured when it no longer oozes sticky glue on your hand. Now you can remove your slime from the water solution.

6. Remove the mixing cups/bowls, sticks and paper towels.

7. Pour the leftover liquid from the cups/bowls down the drain. Dispose of leftover solids in the trash, wash, recycle or dispose of cups & bowls.

How to present it to your group:

1. Pour the glue into cups or bowls ahead of time; you can approximate the amount of glue in the cup. Put a paper towel, popsicle stick and glue cup/bowl down in front of each student.

2. Explain to the students that they are going to combine two substances to create a chemical reaction that will make a completely different substance they will be able to play with. Since we are artists as well as scientists, we will make our new plaything beautiful by coloring it before changing the molecular structure of it.

3. Mixing the colors is an exciting and important part of the lesson. Mixing two colors together to make a third color is often a new experience for younger students. Start by offering primary colors of food coloring or colorant. Explain that they can make their slime red (pink, since it is mixed with white glue), blue, yellow or combine colors to make orange or purple. Additionally, they can see what happens when using all the colors. Mixing colors is fun and exciting; it puts participants at ease and is an important part of the process. Don't underestimate the value of this part of the lesson.

4. Add drops of food coloring to the glue and mix with the popsicle stick. Don't put more than 12 or 15 drops of colors total in the mix. I tell students that if they want only one color, they should let me know and I will add 8-10 drops of that color. Otherwise, I will assume they are mixing colors and put 4-5 drops of each color in their mix. I start with one color and go around to each student with that color and repeat this for each additional color. The children can use their wooden craft stick to mix at any time during the coloring process.

5. Fill your pitcher up with water and put the box of borax next to it. Explain to students that we are now going to create our chemical mixture. Put 2 tablespoons of borax laundry powder in each quart water container, explaining that it is the natural chemical borate that causes the molecular change in the glue. Mix with a spoon, and explain that because the borax does not dissolve in the cool water, it is a suspension. Keep mixing the suspension so that there are as many borax particles at the top of the water pitcher as there are at the bottom.

6. Explain to students that you are going to pour the chemical solution into their cup and the molecular change is going to happen immediately. Their job is to use the craft stick to stir the glue with the chemical water, so as much chemical water as possible contacts with the glue. Tell them not to use their hands to stir until you say so.

7. Pour the chemical/water mix into each cup in an amount equal to the amount of glue. It will immediately start curing the glue. This is the Aha! moment for students and they take immense joy in seeing the chemical change.

8. Stir with the stick first and then use hands to be sure that every part of the glue touches the borax/water solution to cure it. The chemical mix will cure the outside layers of glue, leaving pockets and bubbles of sticky glue. The students can now use their hands to squeeze and mix the glue in the water so that those sticky bubbles are popped and the glue inside gets cured. Hands will get sticky but contact with the borax water mix will cure the glue on their hands and it will easily peel off. It will also come off on the fully cured slime ball when they are handling it. They should not wash their hands in the sink until all the cured glue comes off their hands. If you wash sticky glue hands in the sink, it will only serve to clog the drain and waste water.

9. Allow students to play with the slime on the smooth table surface.

10. Students will delight in sculpting, shaping, mashing, tearing and forming their slime.

11. Students can take their own slime home in a sealed plastic bag or you can combine all the slime in one communal slime bowl/tray to observe and handle in the classroom.

Other things you can do with this project:

1. Put out cookie cutters and playdough tools for children to work with.

2. See how long you can stretch your slime in a continuous string. We have had students create string 36 feet long with 2 ounces of slime.

3. Give students a straw and see if they are successful in blowing large "slime bubbles."

4. Combine everyone's slime in a bowl or a tray and keep it in the classroom. See what happens when you expose it to the elements, freeze it, leave it uncovered, etc. It will become an experiment to check on every day.

The lesson:

The glue is made up of flexible molecules called polymers. They usually slide by each other much like a liquid. Borax mixed with water creates borate ions. The ions link the glue polymers together so they can't flow as easily, creating the rubbery slime substance.

Preschool science version: Allow 15-30 minutes

Preschoolers willing to get their hands sticky can make the slime in individual cups or bowls just as the older students do. This allows the students to pick their own individual color mixing and it accommodates different cognitive stages of development. Three to six students sitting together then put their slime in a communal plastic container and play with it as a group.

At the end of the session, all slime is combined in one container and kept in an airtight container like a bag or a bowl. It can be brought out and played with upon students' request or when the classroom science director considers it an appropriate time for experimenting with the large blob of slime.

Keep your slime on your parents' good side!

If the children are taking their slime home, I let them know that, "9 out of 10 parents will want to throw your slime away." That comment is inevitably met with, "My parents didn't throw mine away last time," to which I reply, "Where is it now?" The response is, "I don't know." I go on to explain that families are afraid the slime will get stuck in the car upholstery, the carpet, and/or the furniture. Do not store it in your toy box or under the bed (this is what children have told me they will do to hide slime from parents).

The best way to keep your slime from being thrown away is to keep it in a plastic container in the refrigerator or freezer. Take it out when you want to play with it and have a smooth table surface to play on. Families are usually happy with this arrangement, and your slime might survive for a long time.

Vocabulary:

Chemical reaction, solution, suspension, polymer molecules, borate ions

Absorbent Water Balls

Scientifically engineered cellulose water balls absorb water and expand to 20 times their original size. Students start out by putting the tiny beads of cellulose in clear plastic cups. They observe them throughout the day and the next day discover that the balls have absorbed the water in the cup and have grown. The balls become jelly-like and are great fun to handle.

When the balls have reached their maximum size, children (and adults) love to play with them. Five to ten minutes of ball-time on a smooth table surface is sufficient. Then put them in individual plastic sandwich bags to take home. Parents are often panicked when they see the bag of balls coming home. Their fears are soothed with the suggestion that the balls be put outside to provide moisture to plants; this is also something the children enjoy doing when they get home.

Materials:

- Cellulose water balls: available in the plant section of variety stores and online
- 9-ounce transparent plastic cups
- Re-sealable sandwich bags
- Water

How to:

- Put cellulose beads in plastic cups and add water.
- Observe and wait 12 hours.

How to present it to your group:

1. Put the cellulose beads in plastic cups: 15-20 per cup is good; yes, the children will be counting to see that it is fair. Write each child's name on their cup.

2. Pass the cups out and explain that the cellulose beads are going to absorb water and grow, but it will take overnight before they are their full size. Urge students to feel the beads and note how small they are.

3. Fill each cup about 3/4 full of water.

4. Children will observe them for a few minutes. Then you should store them where they can't be meddled with.

5. The next day, drain any excess water from the cup before giving the cups to the students.

6. Allow the students to observe and play with the jellied balls before putting them in a plastic bag to take home or releasing the balls into the wild (outside where they can water some plants).

The lesson:

The water balls are made of a very absorbent polymer much like the kind found in disposable diapers. These polymers have amazing absorbency properties because of their ability to fit other molecules (like water) into their structure.

Preschool science version: 5-10 minutes (the first day), 10-20 minutes (the second day)

The first day of observing and feeling the tiny beads and then putting them in water only takes 5-10 minutes. The real fun is observing, playing with and squishing some of the balls when they are done the next day.

On the first day, divide the children into groups of 4-6. Have members of each group observe the water beads and help to put them in a container of water. About 10-15 beads per child is a wonderful way to have them count the beads into the water container. The second day, the groups will be amazed at the change in the beads and enjoy putting their hands in the container.

The children will enjoy the fact that the balls grew and the tactile feel of them. The second-day activity will consist of 10-20 minutes of fun. You can combine all water balls in one large container for a weeklong observation or lead the class outside to place the water balls near the base of some plants to see how quickly they release moisture.

Vocabulary:

Molecules, absorbing, polymer, structure

Bubble Science Formula

Everybody likes making bubbles, but concocting the best bubble mix takes a scientist. This activity lets everyone take part in the science of measuring and mixing of the bubble potion as well as the fun of making and frolicking with bubbles.

I do this activity quite often so I keep a large selection of durable plastic bubble wands handy. You can add a building/creating dimension to the project by constructing your own wands. You will find many good instructions for this online. If you are really spartan in your supply budget, have the children dip hands in the soap mix and blow bubbles through their fingers. Some people love to do this and some will be repelled by getting anything sticky on their hands.

Materials:

- Blue Dawn dish soap (blue works best)

- Water

- Glycerin (you can substitute light corn syrup for glycerin but your mix will be a bit stickier)

- Measuring cup: can be any size as we are doing ratios of 4:1

- Mixing containers: a pitcher works best, for each team to mix solution in (size depends on the size of your measuring cup; you are going to have 5 parts liquid)

- Something to stir with

- A pan to hold bubble mix for you to dip in

- Whatever bubble wands, pipe cleaners, netting or bubble tools available

- A large container to store extra bubble solution. Gallon water jugs work great.

How to:

1. Mix one-part Blue Dawn dish soap with four parts water (distilled is best but tap water is fine too). Use approximately 1-2 tablespoon (s) of glycerin for every cup of soap.

How to present it to your group:

1. Divide your group into teams of 4-6 people.

2. Give each team a measuring cup, a mixing container and something to stir with.

3. Have them divide the measuring jobs so each team member participates.

4. Measure and pour four parts water into the container; four people can each put a part in the mixing container.

5. Measure and pour one part soap with the water.

6. Walk around with the glycerin and a spoon, allowing team members to put the correct amount of glycerin in the mixture.

7. Have each team member give five gentle stirs to the mix; keep foam to a minimum.

8. Pour the mix into the large communal storage container or right into a bubble tray or whatever you are using to put your bubble wands in.

9. Go outside and have fun.

10. We often adhere to the guideline that you can only pop your own bubbles unless someone has given you permission to pop theirs.

The lesson:

Proper measuring and mixing is always important to bubble science. The inside of a bubble is made of air while the skin has three layers: an outside layer of soap, an inside layer of soap and a layer of water in between the soap layers. Your bubble pops when the water layer evaporates. Warmer weather makes your bubble pop quicker. A bubble becomes round because its stretchy "skin" is trying to contract—the air pressure inside is pushing against the "skin" in all directions equally. Glycerin and corn syrup make stronger bubbles because they slow down the evaporation of water in the bubble layer.

Preschool science version: Mixing, 15-20 minutes; playing with bubbles, 15-40 minutes

Have five children in each group. Explain measures and ratios by having 4four students each pour a measure of soap into a container and have one student pour one measure of water. The mixture is made up of five parts soap and water. If you need more bubble mix, do it twice; repetition helps build knowledge. With very young children, it is best for the teacher to add glycerin or corn syrup to avoid messes.

Go outside with your mix and have bubble fun!

Vocabulary:

Molecules, surface tension, evaporation, air temperature, ratios, measure

Exploding Bags

Children love to hear that something is going to explode. Many ask how big the explosion will be, how loud and how dangerous. Some ask with eager anticipation, while others are nervous and need reassurance that the reaction is safe and contained. Once the bags start popping, the children are delighted.

This is an exciting way to watch the pressure of gas produced by the reaction of vinegar and baking soda, causing plastic bags to inflate and explode. People are thrilled by exploding science experiments and this one delivers with non-toxic, fire-free elements.

Materials:

- One-quart plastic food storage bags with slider seal
- White vinegar
- Baking soda

How to:

- Put 3 tablespoons of baking soda in a plastic bag.
- Put 1/3 cup of vinegar in the bag.
- Close it fast!
- Watch the bag inflate until it pops.

How to present it to your group:

1. Give each student a bag and have the teacher put 2-3 tablespoons of baking soda in each bag.

2. Go outside.

3. Explain to students that the vinegar is reacting with baking soda, creating gas, creating pressure, expanding the bag, and eventually exploding.

4. Fill bags with 1/3 to 1/2 cup of vinegar.

5. Watch the bag inflate until it pops!

6. If there is an air leak in the bag, it may inflate but it won't pop. You can then either throw it in the air and it will pop on landing or have the student step on it (with one foot, not two—for safety).

The lesson:

Vinegar is an acid and baking soda (bicarbonate) is a base. The acid–base reaction creates carbon dioxide, a gas. The pressure of the gas created by the chemical reaction (acid–base) pushes against the sides of the bag until the bag breaks at its weakest point.

Preschool science version: demonstration, 10-15 minutes; outside time, 10-20 minutes

Gather your group for a demonstration, talk about what will happen and why. I sometimes demonstrate the "pop" indoors with the bag sitting in a tub that I can hold. The students are reassured that this experiment is safe and they begin to eagerly anticipate their own bag explosion.

After the demonstration, go outside, give each child a bag, put baking soda in each and then put vinegar. Some students will need help closing the bag. Have them lay the inflating bag on the ground and take three steps back so as not to be splashed.

Vocabulary:

Chemical reaction, acid–base reaction, carbon dioxide, gas, inflate

Soda and Mentos Geyser

Anticipation of a geyser is as exciting as watching the geyser itself!

Putting Mentos candy into a bottle of diet cola creates an amazing liquid geyser. The carbon dioxide bubbles in the soda attach themselves to thousands of tiny surface pits in the Mentos candy. The bubbles become numerous, creating gas and rapidly pushing the liquid out of the bottle. The effect is intensified because the heavy Mentos candies sink in the bottle, increasing the number of bubbles produced.

Stop licking the table!

The excitement and anticipation of seeing a geyser of soda pop is a delight for children and adults. Inevitably, some of the students will see it as a waste of sweet drink and minty candy. I recommend quickly gathering the spent soda bottles so children don't grab and attempt to drink the leftover soda and Mentos. Even with the bottles removed, there are students who will go as far as to lick the soda right off the launch pad (usually an outdoor table or bench). If I preface the experiment with the "no licking the launch pad" rule, it only seems to plant the idea. This remains an ongoing concern; you can temper this behavior with the mention of bird droppings on outdoor surfaces.

Materials:

- A 2-liter bottle of diet cola (we use diet because it does not contain sugar and therefore makes less of a sticky mess).

- Mint-flavored Mentos candy (they come in tubes of 14; you need at least 7 for maximum shock and awe).

- Cardboard to make a tube for getting Mentos quickly into the bottle. You can buy a special plastic geyser tube specifically for this experiment from specialty toy stores.

How to:

1. Open your bottle and place it on the ground or on a surface outdoors.

2. Put at least seven Mentos candies into your tube.

3. Drop the Mentos into the bottle of cola. Do this quickly (the reaction is instant).

4. Stand back and enjoy the geyser.

How to have your group make it:

1. Make sure that everyone gets a turn putting Mentos into the tube. With a larger group, we will do multiple bottles, changing the number of Mentos for each bottle and comparing geyser heights. This way all students get an equal chance to put Mentos in the tube.

2. Have students stand back away from the geyser as it can go as high as 20 feet.

The lesson:

Soda pop is full of carbon dioxide gas. The Mentos candy provides a place for the dissolved carbon dioxide to "escape" from the liquid. This process is called nucleation. There are so many little holes on the Mentos (so many places for bubbles to gather) that the escaping gas creates a powerful "geyser."

Preschool science version: outdoors, 15-20 minutes

This is a thrilling demonstration for younger children. Everyone participates by putting a Mentos candy in the tube and witnessing the geyser. Give the explanation, mount the tube on the bottle, have children take turns putting Mentos in the tube, stand a safe distant back and start the geyser!

Vocabulary:

Physical reaction, nucleation, nucleation site, carbon dioxide, geyser

Erupting Volcanoes

An exciting and colorful way to demonstrate the chemical reactions between vinegar and baking soda as well as talking a bit about volcanoes. This is an art project and a science experiment rolled into one. Students decorate their volcanoes indoors and the eruptions happen outdoors.

Materials:

- 16-ounce foam cups: you will need 2 cups per volcano
- White vinegar: about 1 gallon for 15-20 volcanoes each erupting 23 times
- Baking soda: about 16 ounces for 15-20 volcanoes, each erupting 2-3 times
- Food coloring
- Masking tape
- Crayons

How to:

1. Make the volcanoes ahead of time using the foam cups and tape:

2. Mark one cup about 1.5" from the bottom. Cut evenly around the circumference of the cup so you have a tiny cup that is 1.5" tall; this is your baking soda reservoir and the top of your volcano.

3. Turn your second whole cup upside down and tape your 1.5" mini cup to the bottom (flat bottom to flat bottom).

4. Use crayons to decorate the volcano.

5. Fill volcano top ¾ from the top with baking soda.

6. Add drops of food coloring.

7. Slowly pour ¼ cup of vinegar on top of the baking soda.

8. The bubbling "lava" cascades over the top of the "mountain," spilling down in a colorful froth covering everything in its path. Children are delighted; it is like a vinegar and baking soda fireworks display.

How to present it to your group:

1. Put crayons out and give each student a foam and paper volcano.

2. Talk a bit about volcanoes: where are they? Are there any near us? What kind of life might be found on a volcanic mountain? Encourage students to draw things on their volcano that they would expect to find on a volcanic mountain.

3. Take the students outside and have them put their volcanoes on a table or on the ground. You will want them grouped close together although you might need to work on two tables. It is easier for the vinegar pourer and more dramatic to have volcanoes erupting close together. This also allows students to watch others colorful eruptions.

4. Talk about the reaction between baking soda (a base) and vinegar (an acid).

5. Put a tablespoon of baking soda in each volcano.

6. Go around the table offering drops of food coloring to each student. Many will want multiple colors; put 1-3 drops of each color onto the baking soda.

7. When everyone has baking soda and food coloring, you can go around the table pouring vinegar onto the baking soda. Put enough vinegar in to fill the reservoir. Watch the chemical reaction and colorful eruptions.

8. Go around the table a second time with the vinegar only. On the third and fourth eruption, you need to replenish the baking soda and food coloring.

The lesson:

Vinegar and baking soda: This is an example of an acid–base chemical reaction. Vinegar (acid) and baking soda (base) combine to create carbon dioxide (gas). This is what makes all the fizzy bubbles.

Preschool science version:

Younger children will take less time on the indoor coloring part of the volcano than older children. You will probably spend 10-15 minutes on indoor explanation and coloring. Outdoor eruptions last 15-30 minutes depending on the size of your group and the number of times you replenish the baking soda, vinegar and colors.

Vocabulary: Volcano, eruption, lava, chemical reaction, acid, base

. . . .

Cornstarch Slime

This is a "hands-in" slime that is liquid and solid. The cornstarch and water mix creates a substance that can be hard when you squeeze it in your hands and an oozing liquid mud when you release it. Adding color makes it even more interesting.

It was a big relief when it fell off!

I was doing this activity with a particularly energetic group of six- and seven-year-olds. They loved the "slime that is both a liquid and a solid"; the cool colors, the textures and the ooze thrilled them all. In their enthusiasm, the children had spread the mix over a large part of their bodies and clothing. As the activity wound down, my biggest concern was keeping the mess out of the indoor classroom; secondarily, I thought about their parents' car upholstery. Before going inside, we went to the play yard and began a game. The cornstarch began to dry and completely fell off the children and their clothing! I follow each cornstarch slime session with outdoor play and have not been afraid of cornstarch mess since.

Materials:

- Cornstarch
- Large mixing bin or bowl
- Water
- Food coloring

How to:

1. Put the cornstarch in the bowl or bin.

2. Add several drops of coloring.

3. Stir water a little at a time until your mix is no longer powdery. It is a delicate balance between too much water and too little. Start with one cup of water for 16 ounces of cornstarch and then go from there.

4. Play with the mixture; see that it is solid when you squeeze it and an oozing liquid when you let it flow.

How to present it to your group:

1. Set up several bowls or bins with cornstarch; have one bin for every 4-6 students.

2. Use approximately 16 ounces of cornstarch for every 6 students.

3. Set up buckets or bins of water for students to rinse off the cornstarch. This keeps everybody from using the sink and dripping on the floor.

4. Color each bin differently so students can move from bin to bin.

5. Explain how exciting it is to have slime that is both a liquid and a solid. Talk about the reasons for the suspension mix. Remind them that cornstarch is in a lot of the food they eat.

6. As students rinse their hands in the bucket and then go back to the cornstarch bins, the mix gets watery. Have some extra cornstarch available to replenish the slime.

The lesson:

The cornstarch molecules (solids) are suspended in the water (liquid) much like quicksand. The cornstarch molecules slide by each other when you drip them like a liquid. When you tighten your hand on them, they clump together and feel solid.

Preschool science version: Mixing, demonstration and explanation take about 5 minutes. Playing with the slime takes anywhere from 15 to 30 minutes.

Cornstarch and water slime is an engaging textural and tactile experience for preschool students. Divide your class into groups of four and give each group their own bin of slime so that everyone feels it and comments together. This can be done indoors and outdoors but is easier to clean up outside.

Vocabulary:

Suspension, molecules, liquid, solid

Color Mixing Lab

Create an exciting lab for mixing color potions using food coloring and water. This activity encourages the use of lab tools, teaches color fundamentals and engages children in creating their own personal color mixes. There are professional color mixers in the paint, dye and fabric business. I tell the students to look at the colors in their clothing, in the paint on the wall and in every piece of printed material. Each color was created by a person specializing in the science and art of color mixing. This is important work.

This is potion making!

During a five-day summer camp called *Potions, Oohs and Ahhs!* at a time when every elementary school child was talking about the Harry Potter stories, I got an insight into what some children define as potions. My plan was to have students do chemistry experiments where exciting things happen when you mix substances together. On the first day, we made my favorite slime experiment and the children were thrilled, except for one boy who came up to me at the end of class and said, "That was fun but when are we going to mix potions?" I took his constructive criticism to heart and the next day everyone made a rocket and flew it using the chemical reaction of mixing Alka Seltzer and water. After an afternoon of rocket flight, the same boy came to me and said, "I thought this was a potions class!" The third day we set up the color mixing lab. The children were enjoying it very much and mid-way through our lab time the boy came up to me and said, "Now, this is potion making!"

Materials:

- At least four plastic bins; one quart or larger to hold colored water—food storage containers work great. One larger bin works great as a bin to dump used mixes.

- Food coloring or watercolor containing the primary colors red, blue and yellow (more colors are OK as is just clear water)

- Transparent plastic cups for students to mix their colors (9-ounce wide cups are great)

- Pipettes (eyedroppers), syringes or small spoons

How to:

1. Fill bins with water and put food coloring in so you have the primary colors and any others laid out. One set of colors for every 4-6 students works well.

2. Put a "dump bin" at every table for dumping excess water.

3. Give each student one or two plastic cups to mix in.

4. Give each student a pipette, syringe or spoon for transferring colors from the communal bins to their own cups.

How to present it to your group:

1. Talk about what happens when you mix colors: red and blue make purple, red and yellow make orange, yellow and blue make green. Can you make different shades of these colors? What happens when you mix all the colors? What color is the dump bin? What happens when you add that color to another? For many students, color mixing is a new concept.

2. Demonstrate how the pipette and syringe work. Help those students who are struggling with the use of the tools.

3. Clean up spills with good humor.

Extra things to do with this experiment:

1. Have older students chart what their mixes are: 4 parts blue plus 2 parts yellow equals?

2. Give students color examples with markers, crayons or examples from around the room. Can they replicate the colors? Can they chart the amount of each color necessary to copy the color?

The lesson:

This activity epitomizes the scientific method. Students observe, hypothesize, test and repeat the properties of colors. Advanced techniques encourage measurement and recording of data.

Preschool science version: Expect to spend 5 minutes explaining the process and 15-20 minutes mixing colors.

Mixing one color with another and coming up with a third color is often a new experience and an Aha! moment for young children. The concept of red and yellow making orange is awe inspiring if it is their first time. Use tools that are age-appropriate. The syringe is a bit complex for younger children; if the pipette is difficult, the children can always mix with a spoon or small ladle.

Vocabulary:

Primary colors, hypothesis, recording data

Ooey Gooey Lab

This is a sensory and potions experience that delights children with hands-on and hands-in experimentation. Ooey Gooey lab is made up of different stations where children see and feel how various substances mix together, how they react with each other and what it feels like to play with and touch them. Feeling different textures of the mixes and letting them run through your fingers is quite satisfying.

There is a wonderful potential for mess, so I like to do this experience outdoors on dirt or grass with rinsing buckets and towels handy.

Material combinations:

1. **Cornstarch, water, food coloring:** The slime that is both a liquid and a solid is always fun to play with. Combine 16 ounces of cornstarch with approx. 8 ounces of water. Use food coloring to make it look cool. **The lesson:** This is a suspension of a solid (cornstarch) and a liquid (water). They are together but do not absorb each other. That is why when you press on the mix it feels solid because the starch molecules are compressed. When you let it go, the starch and water molecules run freely.

2. **Shaving cream:** Shaving cream has an amazingly silky feel and it smells good. It will make a bit of a mess so make sure to have a rinsing bucket and towels handy before students go inside. You will have to keep replenishing the shaving cream. **The lesson:** Shaving cream is cool because it can exist as a solid, a liquid and a gas. Inside the can, it is a mix of soap and water that is compressed as a gas. When it is sprayed out, it is a solid; eventually, it condenses to a liquid.

3. **Oil and water:** Oil will float on top of the water, and many people delight in moving it around. You can even color the water for an interesting effect and differentiation of color. Use inexpensive vegetable oil. Oil and water is fun to mix in a plastic bottle, much like a lava lamp. This makes it easier to shake and mix, and it keeps oily mess to a minimum. **The lesson:** Oil and water will not mix together because the force of attraction between molecules of the same liquid is stronger than that between the two liquids. If liquids will not mix together, they are immiscible. Oil rises above water because it is denser (has more mass) than water.

4. **Vinegar and baking soda:** Fill the bin or bowl with vinegar and allow students to use a spoon to add baking soda. Observe the reaction between a base and acid as well as noting the smell. You will need to replenish this bin/bowl a few times. **The lesson:** This is an example of an acid–base chemical reaction. Vinegar (acid) and baking soda (base) combine to create carbon dioxide (gas). This is what makes all the fizzy bubbles.

How to present it to your group:

1. Create bins or bowls of ingredient combinations and put them on tables outside. Have enough bins so that your bin to student ratio is about 1:4.

2. Put out rinse buckets and towels. Rinse bucket and towel ratio is about 1:10, but you will need to change the rinse water occasionally.

3. Explain to students the science of each ooey gooey station. Remind them that the main lesson is to experience how things feel.

4. Let them loose to have fun.

Preschool science version:

All parts of the ooey gooey lab are fun to do with your preschool children. Break the activities into 15-20 minute blocks by doing some indoors and some outdoors. The least mess indoors is the oil and water "lava lamp" bottles. Do oil and water bottles indoors for 10-20 minutes, and then take your group outdoors for another 20-30 ooey gooey minutes.

Vocabulary:

Suspension, molecules, solid, liquid, gas, force of attraction, density, mass, chemical reaction, immiscible

CHAPTER 2

FANTASTIC FLYING THINGS

Water Bottle Rocket

Build and launch a rocket that really flies using a water bottle, popsicle sticks, a wine cork, tape, crayons Alka Seltzer tablets and water. This experiment covers Engineering (building the rocket), Art (decorating the rocket) and Science (the chemical reaction between the Alka Seltzer and water).

Materials:

- One 500 mL (16.9 ounce) plastic bottle (the lighter the bottle, the higher the flight)

- Four wood popsicle sticks

- One plastic wine cork (natural cork must be tape wrapped to prevent air leaks)

- Four 1.5-2" pieces of masking tape

- One 12-16-inch piece of duct tape

- Three Alka Seltzer tablets or generic brand (broken in half to make 6 halves)

- 1/4-1/3 cup of water

How to:

1. Empty your bottle, remove the labels and the cap. Insert the cork 1/4-3/8 inches into the neck of the bottle.

2. Decorate 4 popsicle sticks with cool designs using crayons, pencils or pens. Put your name or initials on at least 2 sticks. These will be the legs for your rocket.

3. Put a piece of masking tape at the top of each popsicle stick so it looks like the letter "T." Do this for all 4 sticks.

4. Stand the bottle up on the table with the cork end on the table. With the bottle on the table, attach the sticks by taping them to the side of the bottle, making sure all 4 are level so that the bottle stands without wobbling. Resist the urge to pick the bottle up to accomplish this taping, leave it on the table!

5. Wrap the duct tape around the top of the sticks so they are secured to the bottle. Your rocket should stand straight without wobbling. It is ready to go airborne!

How to launch your rocket:

1. Break 3 Alka Seltzer tablets in half (so they fit through the neck of the bottle). Put the Alka Seltzer into your bottle. Add approximately 1/4-1/3 cup of water to the bottle.

2. Quickly put the cork on the bottle 1/4 to 3/8 inch into the bottle. Stand the bottle on the ground or on your launch pad. Stand back and watch it fly!

How to have your group make it and launch it:

You are going to construct your rocket indoors at tables or desks and then launch it outdoors. The key to success is to have your prep done ahead of time and have your students construct the rocket one step at a time. You can construct and launch the rockets in one session or divide it into two activities. It depends on your class time and the ages and ability of your group

Making the Rocket

1. First prep the bottles by emptying them of liquid, getting rid of caps and cutting off any labels. Insert the corks 1/4"-3/8" into the bottle, put them aside.

2. Put 4 popsicle sticks and 4 pieces of masking tape at each student's place on the table or desk. Put crayons, pencils or pens where students can reach them.

3. Bring the students to the table and have them decorate their sticks any way they like, making sure that they put their name or initials on at least two sticks. I usually allow 3-4 minutes for decorating. If students are not finished, assure them they can decorate the legs some more once the rocket is built.

4. Have students put tape on the end of each stick like the letter "T."

5. Demonstrate taping the 4 sticks to the bottle while the bottle is standing cork end down on the table. Then show them how you will come around and put the duct tape on. It is important that you demonstrate how the sticks go on while keeping the bottle and sticks level and on the table.

6. Distribute the bottles and have the students adhere the sticks to their bottles. Younger students will require assistance with this step. Have an adult or older helper go around and "duct tape" the rocket legs once they are attached. Students should leave their finished rocket at their table until it is time to go outside for launch.

 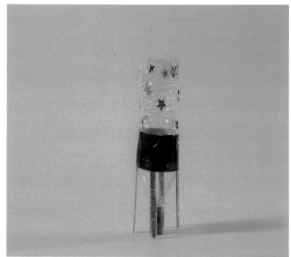

Launching the Rocket

1. Have students come outside with their rockets. Assign a number to each student (i.e. 1,2,3…)

2. Have a launching pad: a flat surface or on the ground

3. Talk about the chemical reaction between the water and the Alka Seltzer ingredients.

4. Talk about safety: stay back from the rocket while it is loaded. Do not put your face above the rocket. Never point the cork at anyone because it can cause serious hurt. Always watch a loaded rocket, if it falls over students should avoid the cork and the instructor should immediately right it. The pressurized cork is a serious projectile.

5. Let students know that only the person who owns the rocket can catch it or pick it up after launch. The rocket owner must retrieve their own rocket and the cork.

6. Call the first student number.

7. Have the student hold the cork while you put 6 Alka Seltzer halves and approximately 1/4- 1/3 cup of water in the bottle.

8. The student hands you the cork and you cork the bottle immediately.

9. Give it a slight shake and put it on the launch pad.

10. Watch it fly!

Other things you can do with this project:

1. Launch the rockets at an angle and guess the trajectory (physics). You can do this by placing it in a bin or a box that gives it some angle.

2. Demonstrate the power of pressure by shooting the cork out of the bottle like a projectile. Make sure it is not pointed at any person or the ground. We often shoot "pop flies" into a field by pointing the rocket up and letting the cork shoot.

The lesson:

When water is added to the Alka-Seltzer tablet a chemical reaction occurs, creating bubbles of carbon dioxide gas. More gas is produced, creating pressure inside the bottle until there is enough force to overcome the seal of the cork. The pressure exerts enough force to launch the rocket high into the air. Students will observe that a lighter rocket will go higher and the flight pattern (trajectory) will change according to the angle of the launch (which way it is pointed).

Preschool science version:

The making of rockets is a 15-20-minute indoor activity and the launching is a 20-25-minute outdoor project.

Instead of having every child make their own rocket, you can divide up into groups of 4 students with each group making one rocket. Each group member will decorate a popsicle leg and participate in building the rocket. Each group member will put a piece of Alka Seltzer tablet in the rocket under the supervision of the instructor in charge of rockets.

The rockets that are made can be saved as classroom rockets to be launched again at another time.

Vocabulary: Chemical reaction, trajectory, force, gas, pressure

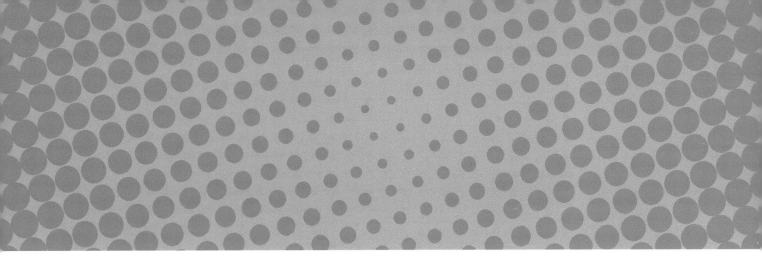

Balloon Line Propulsion

Create a balloon track where balloons speed along propelled by their own air jets. Compare the speed of large balloons versus small, round versus tubular, etc. How far can your balloon go on its own power? You can create several lines and have dramatic balloon races.

Materials:

- Balloons of different shapes and sizes
- Fishing line (monofilament)
- Plastic drinking straws: cut into 2" lengths
- Masking tape

How to:

1. String the fishing line between two points 10-30 feet apart. String the line through your straw piece before you secure it. Make the line as tight and straight as you can. Indoors we have used sturdy desks and chairs as securing points.

2. Attach a piece of masking tape to your straw so that there are two sticky ends available for attaching the balloon. These ends will stick to and hold the balloon. You will be changing the tape frequently.

3. Blow your balloon up, hold the end so air does not escape. Secure the balloon to the masking tape attached to the straw.

4. Let it go and watch it race.

How to present it to your group:

1. Stringing the lines takes the most time so do it before your group arrives unless they are old enough to help you.

2. Explain how the release of pressurized air creates energy that propels the balloon along the track. The nylon line and the straw keep friction to a minimum allowing the balloon to travel fast.

3. It is fun to have some lines going one way and others going perpendicular at different heights. The point at which the balloons pass each other is always fun to watch.

4. With a large group you will have to take turns and change the balloon for each person (hygiene). This requires a deft hand at replacing tape often.

The lesson:

When the balloon is blown up the air is pushing on the sides of the balloon. When you are pinching the narrow opening closed, high-pressure air inside can't escape. Releasing the neck of the balloon allows the pressurized air to escape, creating thrust that powers the balloon along the track.

Vocabulary

Thrust, pressure, high pressure, pressurized, propulsion, physics

Giant Paper Gliders

If you like to construct beautiful things and then fly them, this project is for you. Your students will create giant durable paper airplanes, make them beautiful and enjoy learning and playing with the aerodynamics of flying. This is engineering, building, art and physics in one tremendously fun indoor/outdoor project.

Materials:

- 22" x 14" white poster paper
- Crayons or markers
- Duct tape

How to:

Begin folding the paper

1. **Hot dog bun:** fold paper lengthwise

2. **House:** fold 2 corners to the center line

3. **Rocket:** fold both sides to the center line

4. **Unicorn:** fold both wing sides together

5. **Jet:** fold wings down from tip to tail so the edge of the wing lines up with the bottom edge

6. Wrap duct tape on the tip to add weight and protect during crash landings.

7. Begin decorating your plane.

8. Put your name on it

9. Use crayons and markers to make it look as cool as you want it to be.

Go outside and fly!

How to present it to your group:

1. Folding large sheets of rigid paper can be challenging for small hands. I will often make the first fold (hot dog bun) on each sheet before we begin. This way the paper does not crowd the tables and desks and it insures a straight fold in the beginning that makes the entire process smoother. You will need to help those with smaller hands on every fold.

2. Once the paper is folded, I urge the children to decorate the plane in any way they like. I remind them that many commercial airlines decorate the outside of their planes completely. Some students make military insignia while others draw windows with people looking out. Some of my favorite designs are just abstract and beautiful patterns and colors. The only requirement is that they put their name on their plane somewhere.

3. As the students are decorating their plane, I will come around and wrap the tip in duct tape. This gives it extra weight for longer flights and protects the tip during landings. I use about 6 inches of duct tape to double wrap the first 3" of the tip.

4. Safety: Before we begin flying I explain that they are the pilots responsible for where the plane goes. The plane can hurt someone if it hits them in the wrong place. It is the duty of the pilot to make sure that nobody is in the flight path of the plane. No flying your plane at other people!

5. Aerodynamics: Demonstrate to the students that the direction their plane will fly is determined by the angle of the plane at launch. If the tip of the plane is angled way up, it will go straight up and then fall. If it is angled down, it will simply go into the ground. If the plane is kept straight, it will fly straight. It is also worth talking about which direction the wind is coming from and urge them to experiment to see what happens when they fly into the wind, with the wind and sideways to the wind.

6. Go outside and have fun!

7. We will often set-up flying games where students attempt to fly their planes through hoops or the openings in our desk chairs.

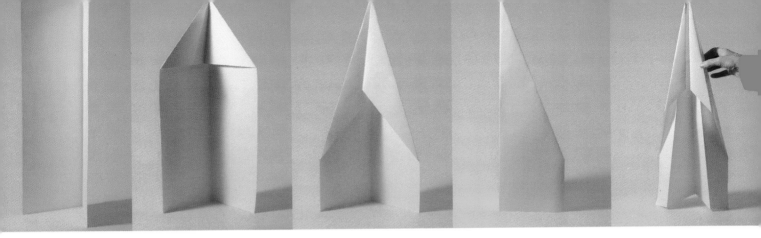

The lesson:

The folding and creating of a flying paper jet is a bit of creative engineering, as is the addition of duct tape for durability and enhanced flight. Decorating the plane with crayons, markers, stickers, ribbon and anything else makes a wonderful art project. The actual flying of the planes gets the children thinking about the physics of flight; direction, angle, wind, thrust, etc. This project incorporates science, art and engineering and culminates in a fun outdoor activity and a cool project to take home.

Preschool version:

Use 8.5" × 11" letter size card stock to make the gliders. The smaller plane is easier for preschoolers to color and to fly. Make the first fold (hot dog bun) yourself so that everything starts out straight. Most of the children will need help with folds and will have a sense of humor about the fold names.

Once the planes are made, decorated and taped it is time to have outside flying time. Many of the children will have never flown a paper airplane so take time to demonstrate and provide plenty of flight training.

Vocabulary:

Thrust, angle, wind direction, trajectory

Hovering Hot Air Balloons

This flying experiment is awesome indoors and outdoors. You use helium balloons, ribbon and foam cups to simulate hot air balloon flight. Students add and subtract weight to get their hot air balloon to hover and travel around.

Materials:

- One helium balloon with a 6-8-foot ribbon attached.
- One 8-ounce foam cup
- Crayons or markers
- Small paper wads, twigs or leaves for weight

How to:

1. Decorate your cup and make it look beautiful.

2. Use a pencil or pen to punch 2 parallel holes (one on each side of the cup) just below the rim.

3. String the balloon ribbon between the two holes and pull it through until the balloon is about 1.5 feet from the cup.

4. Tie the ribbon onto the tied balloon opening so that the cup appears secured to the balloon on two sides. There should be several feet of ribbon as a leash attached to the tied end of the balloon.

5. Add and subtract weight to get the balloon to hover at one level. Gently blow on it to get it to travel around the room or the yard.

6. You can park your balloon by putting heavier weights in it.

How to present it to your group:

1. Create a sample hot-air balloon by decorating a cup to look like an old fashion basket complete with furnace and people. You will need your sample when explaining what is going to happen.

2. Talk about how hot air balloons rise by having the temperature of the air in the balloon warmer than the air around it. Explain how the balloon operator would create warm air to get the balloon to rise and then attempt to hover and travel on air currents.

3. Be specific explaining how they can first figure out just the right weight to get the balloon to hover (stay at one level). As they travel around the room or yard they will notice that air temperature changes and will affect their balloon differently.

4. Start the activity indoors so students get the hang of hovering and controlling their balloons. After a while you can bring the activity outdoors.

5. Be sure to secure strings/ribbons to the student's wrists when they are outdoors. Have some extra balloons to replace the inevitable escapee.

6. Outdoors, we have enjoyed adding ribbon, yarn or string and extending the length of the leash. Flying a balloon with a 20-foot leash is quite different from flying with a 6-foot leash. Have fun experimenting with different lengths.

The lesson:

Hot air rises because it is lighter (less dense) than colder air. Helium is lighter than air and a helium balloon acts much the

same as a balloon full of hot air would in our hot air balloon experiment. The buoyant force of the helium causes it to rise in the lighter air. The buoyant force is neutralized by adding weight to the balloon basket (foam cup) reminding us of the force of gravitational pull.

Preschool version:

The preschool lesson is in adding objects to the cup to control the rise of the balloon. Start by attaching foam cups to a few balloons. Divide your children into groups of 2-4 who will work well together. Have each group add or subtract weight to the cup to get their balloon to hover.

This activity will last 15-25 minutes indoors or out.

Vocabulary

Weight of air, buoyant force, gravitational pull, balance, density

Rocket Balloons

Rocket balloons are always a hit with their screaming and spirited flight patterns. Narrow air holes give them powerful and long-lasting propulsion energy while the odd shapes make them fly in erratic ways making them as unpredictable as living creatures. Children love the unpredictable nature and will fly them for a long time.

Materials:

- Rocket balloons—many come with blow up straws
- Hand-held balloon pump—save your lungs!
- Rocket balloons to replace poppers and escapees

How to:

1. Take a balloon
2. Inflate it
3. Point it upwards to fly
4. Retrieve; repeat
5. Always clean up broken and popped balloon carcasses

How to present it to your group:

1. This is primarily a way to have fun outdoors but it is always good to point out the physics of propulsion and the aerodynamics of shape. The balloon flies so far and so fast because the hole where the air escapes is small and so the pressurized air being released creates energy. The balloon flies in crazy patterns because of the shape (the long balloon often has a slight arc that will steer it and spin it.

2. This activity is best done in an open space so that balloons are not eaten by trees. Meadow grass can also pop balloons but it is great fun to launch your balloon parallel to the ground and watch it creep along the ground.

3. Be sure to have extra balloons because you will lose quite a few.

The lesson:

What sets these balloons apart from regular balloons is the small air opening and the irregular and oblong shape of the balloon. Children learn that trapped air exerts pressure, pushing the balloon along. They will also notice that air escaping through the small opening often creates sound much like human whistling. The irregular shape creates random flight patterns unlike a straight glider plane or our balloon on a straight fishing line experiment.

Preschool version:

Your youngsters will be thrilled by the rocket balloons. If you do this indoors, you can sit in a circle and explain how trapped air can create power. Blow a balloon up, assign one person to stand up to follow it and pick it up when it lands. Repeat for everyone in the group. If your group is larger than 12 it is better to split the group up. Outdoors you can blow balloons up and hand them to children in turn. Having more adults makes this an easier job. Some children will need help figuring out how to pinch the balloon shut before letting it go.

Vocabulary: Velocity, air pressure, physics of flight, sound

CHAPTER 3

FORTS: CARDBOARD CITY

Cardboard City: Private Houses

Children are gleeful when they get their very own box (house). Most of them will immediately get in their box, open the window and grin! Some are so happy to have their own space, they will simply go in and enjoy the solitude and ownership. These moments are the thrill of childhood cardboard box play.

All citizens of Cardboard City get their own house that can double as a business as well. The houses are made of extra-large moving boxes you can buy at the local home improvement store. Children love cardboard boxes, especially ones that they can fit into. On the first day of cardboard city, each citizen is given their own house (box), allowed to find a neighborhood for it and begins to decorate and customize it to their own preferences.

I learned the hard way that having your own house is important. At the first ever cardboard city class, I had a utopian view of communal building, living and sharing. It started out fine except that one or two students did most of the building construction. When everybody started to move in to the buildings, the children who did most of the construction complained bitterly that they had done the building and the others had no right to occupy what they had made. The argument became so heated that a girl (the older sister of one of the builders) grabbed a box, made a sign and declared herself the village lawyer. She charged $5 for mediation and problem solving. Her brother was less than impressed but the other children were thrilled and her lawyer business prospered for the rest of the week.

Materials:

- Extra-large moving box: 22" × 22" × 22"
- Box cutters (for instructor, not students)
- Student art supplies (paper of many colors, crayons, markers, scissors, tape, glue)
- Clear carton-sealing tape

How to:

1. Seal the bottom of the box; tape all seams but leave the top flaps open.

2. Use the box cutters to cut a door big enough for children to enter. First cut a 1" hole to act as a doorknob then cut three sides to make the door. Make a straight line indentation (score) the hinged side for easier opening.

3. On another side, cut a transom window (one that is cut on 3 sides and hinges on the bottom edge) this opens out and provides a tray to display things if they open a store or restaurant. The transom window should be about 8" × 10".

4. The new building owner can find a location for their building and begin customizing it.

How to present it to your group:

1. Tape, seal and cut the boxes before starting the lesson. Have them ready in the room or space that will be used.

2. Have art supplies set up in the space where the boxes are—inside or outside.

3. Explain to students that today is when they are going to be introduced to their building and start decorating it.

4. Put students' names on the boxes before you bring the students in.

5. Lead them into the space, have them find their building, find a spot and begin decorating.

The lesson:

Children get to think about and act on how they want to decorate their house, what kind of business they might want to start and where they want their house to be located. Decorating your house is a large creative art venture. Thinking about your business and what you might like to create for it requires complex thinking and some self-reflection. Some children prefer working with others and will create cooperative projects, while others like to act alone.

Cardboard City: Community and Commerce

Students feel immense pride when a product or service they created is bought by someone else. Knowing that someone else thinks well enough of your work to pay for or trade for it is quite satisfying to all of us. Many will tell me gleefully each time they make a sale.

As creativity and commerce begin, your city will start to take form. Public buildings are being created out of large boxes and citizens start making stores, restaurants, farms and other enterprises using their private building and things they have made at the art table. You might find a pet shop selling paper animals, a flower shop, multiple restaurants, farm products, a gym and even a blacksmith shop. Each citizen is given a fixed amount of pre-printed official paper money (usually 10-20) to spend as they please. If they want to earn more money they open a business and create something or work for someone else's business. The children are always eager and excited to begin.

Materials:

- Large moving or appliance boxes for creating public buildings. These are sometimes found at your local appliance store.

- Computer generated cardboard city dollars (I use address label templates on green paper)
- Plenty of art supplies for creating products, business signs and embellishing boxes.

How to present it to your group:

1. Explain to students that they will each receive a set amount of money each day to spend. If they want to make more money, they should open a business or work for a business. They do not have to make more money if they are happy with their daily stipend.

2. It is important to emphasize the idea of buying things from your neighbor so they will buy from you.

3. Emphasize the importance and fun of making things at the art table, showing them to your neighbors and selling them.

4. Explain economics by reminding them what the daily pay is, and what kind of prices someone making $15 per day can pay for things (usually $1-$5)

5. Ask students what they plan to make or do. Advertise for them and always make sure the teacher, helpers and any visitors to the city have plenty of money to spend.

6. Buy something from all who create offerings but don't overpay. The younger students are often loath to spend their money so it is often up to you to stimulate the economy.

Vocabulary:

Wages, prices, commerce, economy, community, service business, product business.

The lesson:

Children learn to work cooperatively in creating communal spaces and in creating an economy that has benefits for everyone. They learn about the quid-pro-quo exchange of services, products and money. Economic lessons include the laws of supply and demand, proper pricing of goods and the concepts of marketing and advertising. Basic math is necessary.

The making of products to sell is a great art lesson; the creation of large cardboard structures is an additional lesson in engineering and building.

Cardboard City – Communal Buildings and civic events

The joy in this part of the activity is creating, sharing and participating in a make-believe world that works just like the real world. Children love it when the library, museum and theater work like real ones do.

A city needs vibrant public buildings and events. Buildings can be made of large appliance boxes or multiple moving boxes. I have even bought moving boxes in bulk and used them as building blocks to create large structures. When the session was over, I broke them down for easy storage and used them a second and third time. Having tall boxes that fit several people at a time brings reality to the city. The buildings become city hall, libraries, museums and performance spaces.

We do not allow crime in Cardboard City, there is no jail and no police force. There are always a few students who watch a lot of television and think it might be fun to be a criminal. It may start out fun for them but not so much for those who are being stolen from. If you allow petty crime, you will be faced with multiple complaints and many tears. Some students will want to form a police force and create a jail to imprison alleged criminals; the police often detain the wrong suspects and can sometimes turn cruel. Policing and jails created more complaints and tears than the crimes themselves. Better to ban crime and punishment, it is a utopian notion but it saves all citizens (and those in charge) much heartache.

Materials:

- Appliance boxes or multiple boxes taped together
- Box cutters: for large doors and elaborate windows
- Art Supplies: for signs and décor

- Carton tape and/or duct tape

How to:

1. Set your large cardboard buildings in a central part of the city.

2. Use the box cutters to cut large doors and multiple windows.

3. Make signs designating the buildings as: City Hall, Library, Museum, Theater, etc.

How to present it to your group:

1. Explain that everyone is welcome in the public buildings and nobody can be excluded.

2. City hall can be where you distribute the daily money.

3. The museum can buy pictures and art from citizens and display it.

4. You can have books in the library and check them out to citizens.

5. Schedule a variety show at the theater. Several members of your group will have a talent they want to share. We have had musicians, singers, dancers and comedy acts. The instructor should make sure that audience members are always respectful to performers. A surefire way to get full attendance at your performance events is to charge admission (split between performers and organizers) but give each audience member a treat of a popsicle, otter/freeze pop or something else irresistible as part of the ticket price.

The lesson:

The lesson is about using your talents to create something that is shared by everyone. Students will find that public buildings that benefit the group also benefit the individual. A student who performs at a talent show will enjoy the stage and get part of the ticket money. The audience gets to watch a show and maybe have a popsicle (performers get popsicles too).

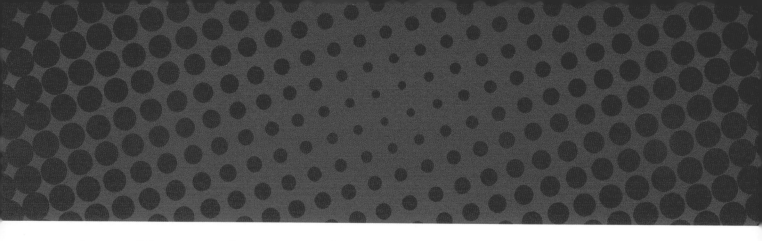

Cardboard Arcade Games

Hole Toss and Mini Basketball

Making your own cardboard arcade game is a wonderful creative art project and a simple engineering project culminating in a toy that provides hours of fun games indoors and out. The most joyful moments I have observed are the satisfaction a child gets when they make a hole or basket they did not expect to make. Children have also taken much pride when their game is popular with fellow students.

The arcade game is made of one half of a standard square shipping box that can be bought anywhere boxes are sold. Each half is a ball toss game on one side and a basketball game on the other.

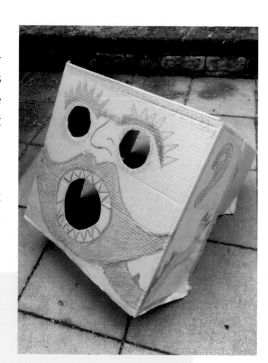

Materials:

- Large square moving box: I use 22" × 22" × 22" from Home Depot
- Clear packing tape
- Box cutters or razor
- 16-ounce foam, paper or plastic cup: for basketball hoop
- Light balls, pinecones or beanbags: for both games

- Crayons, markers and other art supplies to decorate the box
- Paper arcade tickets: handmade or store bought (optional)

How to:

1. Open the flat box and cut down one side so it becomes a sheet with four panels. Each panel is a square (or rectangle) with a flap on each end (top and bottom).

2. Cut the sheet in half so each half has two panels and four flaps.

3. Stand one of the large panels up so it is at a 90-degree angle from the other large panel. Fold the flaps on one side 90 degrees toward the inside – securely tape them to each other and to the large panel. Do the same for the other side flaps.

For Mini Basketball: Cut the bottom out of a foam cup so your ball will fit through easily, this will be your basketball hoop. Tape the cup about midway up on your large box panel so the taped flaps provide "sides" for your "court." Use your art supplies to decorate the court any way you like.

For Hole Toss game: Stand the taped box up so it sits with the large panels angled out, much like a sandwich board. Cut 3 round holes of varying sizes on one of the large panel sides. Use the side without the basketball hoop the holes will appear on the floor of your "court." Make them large enough for your beanbags, balls or pine cones to fit through. Making it through the smaller hole is worth more points than the larger. Decorate your arcade game any way you like. You might even give it a name and a theme as so many game makers do.

How to present it to your group:

Cut the flat boxes ahead of time and cut the round holes for Hole Toss while the box is flat. This is the most efficient way if you are working with a large group. You can tape them ahead of time as well.

It is fine if you prefer your students to engineer all steps. They can even draw the hole circles if an adult does the cutting.

Let the students know this is an ongoing art project. They can choose and draw a theme for the hole toss game and create an arena for basketball.

Once the art is finished, you will hand out balls, bean bags or pinecones. The students will take their games to the playing area and practice playing. Urge them to play other students games and have fun.

If you are using arcade tickets, hand them out after 5 minutes of practice and have students designate the number of tickets they will charge to play a game and how much they will award for each basket or hole made. This can be a difficult mathematical calculation for people to make. I usually suggest they charge 1-3 tickets to play and pay off 1-3 tickets for holes made. This can be adjusted by moving the throwing line.

The lesson:

Students are engineering two functions (games) by modifying a cardboard box. Decorating the basketball arena and hole toss game are large canvas art projects. Playing the games develops coordination, strategy and focus. Working with the ticket awards requires math calculations. Students also must cooperate by playing other people's games and allowing others to play theirs.

Preschool version:

Construct an arcade box for every 4 to 6 students. The first part of the project is having each group of 4-6 use crayons to decorate their arcade game. Explanation and coloring will usually take 10-15 minutes depending on supervision.

The second part is playing the games. Have a playing area inside or out where the different games can be spread out. Children take turns playing other groups games and being the attendant for theirs. Playing will last 10-20 minutes. The boxes can be flattened and stored for future use in the classroom by slitting the tape and folding the box.

CHAPTER 4

BUILDING

Build and Take Apart (Take Apart and Build)

This is a skill-building activity that allows students to "see" technology (circuits, etc.), understand assembly and learn to use tools. They also get a chance to see what makes some of their favorite toys, games and electronic devices work. I have done this project with electronic toys and other electronics like phones, faxes, computers, printers and more. Children seem to relate best to toys so that is what I use most. Creativity really kicks in when students begin to make their own things out of parts. You will see elaborate "steampunk" inventions and macabre characters that appear to be straight out of the *Toy Story* movie series.

Materials:

- Old electronics (working or not): one item for every 2-3 students
- Screwdrivers: both Phillips and regular clutch head. Small Phillips head will be the most used. Consider getting a set of tiny screwdrivers as well
- Pliers, hammer, side cutters
- Battery disposal box

- Plastic sandwich bags to hold screws and parts
- Masking tape and duct tape (because sometimes they are the best building material)
- Small cardboard box

How to:

1. Have a toy and tools at your station.

2. Remove the batteries from your toy. Store or dispose of them properly.

3. Use your tools to take your toy apart and dis-assemble it as much as you want.

4. Keep the screws and small parts in your plastic bag.

5. Use the parts to create something else – it can be an imaginary machine with parts taped to a box or you can re-assemble a car with new chassis and wheels. The main thing is to use your imagination and the parts that you salvaged.

How to present it to your group:

1. Assign teams of 2-4 students to each toy and tool station. All toys are not created equal so we sometimes have teams pick a number out of a bag and they are assigned to that toy. This adds a dimension of fun to the day.

2. Talk to students about how the items that they take for granted can often contain very advanced technology. Let them know that they are taking the toy apart and salvaging the parts to create their own imaginary technological invention.

3. Have students first remove any batteries and put them in a proper disposal place.

4. Students will start dis-assembling. Remember that tool skills are a learned thing; many of the students need help getting things apart. Remind them to put screws and small parts in bags.

5. The teams can either build something new together or divide the parts and each work separately.

6. Give each inventor a box, their parts, access to tape and see what they come up with.

The lesson:

Learning to use tools properly and keeping track of parts is an important skill. Seeing the working mechanical and technical insides of objects that we take for granted is a mind-opening experience for both children and adults.

Vocabulary:

Circuits, computer chips, screwdrivers, springs, wiring

Small House Diorama

Construct a mini version of any building. It may be a house, a store, an office, a factory or a farm. Each student gets a small cardboard box that already has a pre-cut door and window. Students use material from the art area and whatever else you lay out (pieces from electronic take apart? – foam scraps, egg cartons, etc.). They decorate and furnish their building in whatever way they like. We often use this activity as a prelude to Cardboard City week.

Materials:

- Small cardboard box: approx. 10" × 10" × 5" or small enough to be manageable on desk or table
- Box cutters
- Student art supplies: scissors, paper, crayons, markers, glue, tape
- Interesting recycled stuff: foam, egg cartons, cardboard, nuts, bolts, screws, wires

How to:

1. Seal the bottom of the box but leave the top flaps open.

2. Use the box cutters to cut a door in the side of the box by cutting 3 sides of the door and scoring the side that hinges.

3. Cut one or two windows into the side.

4. Decorate your box.

How to present it to your group:

1. Make boxes and cut doors and windows before the lesson starts.

2. Spend several minutes talking about different ideas for creation and have the children come up with ideas so the whole class is excited and has direction.

3. Have students use their imagination to think of all the kinds of buildings they could create.

4. Show them ways that they might make furniture, people, pets or machines with the art supplies and material available.

5. We often do this activity as a prelude to building larger cardboard structures that the children can fit in to.

6. These dioramas can also be created around themes that your group is studying

The lesson:

The construction of a diorama exercises creative art skill, engineering and planning. If you assign a theme (science, technology, historical periods, etc.) it takes on that dimension as well

Lego Float Challenge

This is an amazing fun time with Legos, a plastic wading pool and some air and water squirting tools. The children get very excited as they build their boat and speculate on its ability to float. They are thrilled when it is their turn to propel the boat across the pool and some of them like the festive atmosphere of audience members cheering on others. Quieter people will stay away from the loud crowd if it is not their boat's turn.

Students practice construction with Legos, learn about floatation (what does and what doesn't) and discover ways to propel things on, under and through water. This is best done in warm weather and is always exciting and fun for everyone involved.

Preface the lesson with a statement that humor is imperative in this Lego build. Remind the children that sometimes the most successful bit of fun is with a boat that sinks or floats lopsided. Remind your students that success in this project often means getting the biggest laugh and amusing the spectators. People love to laugh at unexpected occurrences and they are not laughing at the person who built the boat but rather at the antics the boat went through to get to the finish line.

Materials:

- Legos
- A small plastic wading pool
- Tape: to mark the start and finish lines
- Something that blows air: a hollow pipe, a balloon pump, etc.
- Something that blows water: A large squirt device, a balloon pump, etc.

How to present it to your group:

1. Explain that there will be a time limit for each person to build a Lego creation that floats. Your task is to propel it from the start to the finish using one of the propulsion tools.

2. Everybody must start building at the same time. Do not allow testing in the pool or in the classroom.

3. When the building is done, assign each person a number and assemble everyone around the pool. Set up boundary lines so only the floater/boater is within one foot of the pool. The floater/boater will need space to maneuver.

4. Remind everyone that success has nothing to do with floating, some of the best boats sink. The object is to get it to touch the finish line tape. Lopsided boats and sinking boats are what makes this activity fun. If you made your fellow boaters laugh, then you are a winner.

5. Call the first boater/number. Give them a choice of propulsion tools to use, they can switch tools in the middle of their run, they can even use their own breath to propel the vessel. The only rule is that they **cannot touch the boat** with a tool or any part of their body. If they do, they must go back to the start line. If the boat sinks, they can propel it with water pressure or air pressure underwater.

6. When they have successfully reached the finish line (and they all will), they should put their boat on a drying area and cheer their friends on.

The lesson:

Lego boat float is a lesson on building and creating, engineering something that might float, the physics of propulsion, resilience (if your boat flounders) and humor.

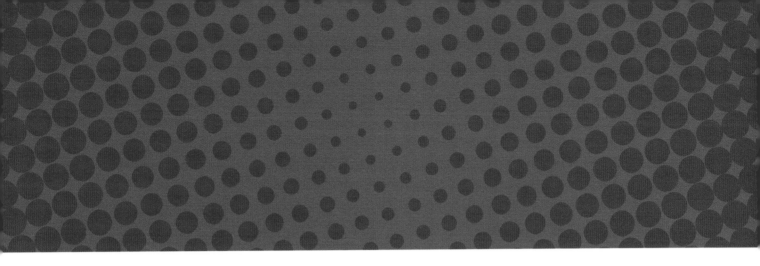

Lego Team Challenge with Stories

This is Lego brick play that allows students to exercise their building, engineering, teamwork, imagination, story-telling and listening skills. Some children like building in cooperation with their friends and make it one of their favorite social activities. Others do not like the group dynamic and prefer solitary building and minimal interaction.

There will be students who love to speak and tell a story about their creation and others who absolutely do not like speaking to a group. The respectful thing to do is to honor all styles of interaction.

The only thing that is universal to all participants is the enjoyment of Lego building.

Your students will look forward to this and when it goes well, there is nothing better. You can occasionally award prizes such as stickers or treats to every team and participant.

Materials:
- A large Lego collection
- Slips of folded paper with 2 part themes written on them (i.e. Castle and Dragon, Zoo and Hippopotamus, Farm and Animals, etc. etc.)

How to present it to your group:
1. Assign students to compatible groups of 2-4.

2. Explain that each group will select a piece of paper with a theme. Their team will be tasked with creating a Lego build that relates to that theme. There will be a time limit (usually 25 minutes).

3. At the end of the time, each team will have 2 minutes to tell the story of what is happening in their creation. Each member will get 30 seconds to speak but can transfer their time to another team member if they like. Some people like to speak and others don't; this should be respected. The other teams should make the effort to be respectful listeners.

4. The team can build one thing together or each person can build a part or they can just build with their own flow.

5. The themes are guidelines; if you draw Zoo and Hippo you could have a space zoo with hippo ship pilots. Use your imagination and tell it in your story.

6. Builders should be sparing when gathering Legos. You should only take what you need for that moment. Grabbing and stockpiling extra pieces is not allowed.

7. Alert the teams when there is 10 minutes left and 5 minutes left. Excess debris must be cleared from their area before the story-telling starts.

The lesson:

Lego challenge teaches students how to work in a team. You can work together on a build or in a parallel fashion but always cooperate with and speak to your fellow team members. It is a good example of developing imagination and storytelling.

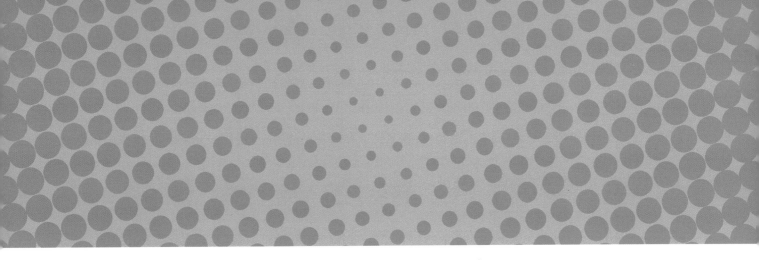

Free Block: Free Build Jamboree

Fitting pieces together, gathering, building and breaking are all joy points for children playing blocks.

Putting as many non-interlocking blocks out as you can for free play releases young builder's limitations and thrills them to no end. I have a few of many kinds of blocks that don't snap together. Wood, foam, plastic, plain and painted blocks. In addition, I have buckets full of corks, paper plates, plastic cups and cardboard for construction. This activity lays everything out and invites children to an open play building jamboree. They combine materials and make creations that they might not get a chance to during more regulated or singular type block play.

Materials:

- As many block sets as you are willing to put out.
- Paper or plastic plates
- Paper or plastic cups
- Pieces of foam
- Cardboard
- Corks

How to present it to your group:

1. Put the blocks and materials on the floor or on tables.

2. Explain to children that they can build anything they want with any building material.

3. Strike a deal with them stating that at the end of play, they will put the blocks or materials back in the section they took them from. Also emphasize that all blocks are to be shared and that is why you might have to build your masterpiece out of several types of blocks.

4. Enjoy your time, referee disputes.

The lesson:

Block building can contribute to every level of child development. Each child will get something valuable out of playing with blocks depending on their own stage of development. Young children learn about shapes, colors and size while older children engage in problem solving and creativity of various levels. Every child in the group practices sharing and cooperation while playing blocks with others; even in parallel playing.

Preschool version:

Most preschool classrooms and homes with preschoolers have many block sets. It is a pleasant experience for children to work on building at the same time as others. All developmental stages will be represented and many young children like to watch older children build. I use block play as a transition activity between projects or when we are waiting for our food to bake in the oven.

CHAPTER 5

PHYSICAL SCIENCE

Marble Runs

Having your marble successfully stay on the track and completing a circuit is exciting. Students are often thrilled when they combine tracks and create large runs.

Marble runs are popular toys in our classroom. This experiment allows students to create their own marble runs with foam pipe insulation and masking tape. Students tape the foam tracks to the walls, the tables, chairs and even themselves. You can also break into groups to combine materials and make larger and more elaborate tracks.

Materials:

- Foam pipe insulation: 6" × 1" is common but you can use numerous sizes
- Masking tape or blue painters tape
- Marbles

How to:

1. Cut some of the pipe insulation in half, length wise to create tracks. Leave some pieces as tubes. Have some 6" lengths and some 3" lengths; cut them down further if desired.

2. Create tracks, runs and drops by taping the foam to the walls, chairs, tables and seeing how marbles move through. You can even wrap track around your body and create a spiral run.

How to present it to your group:

1. Talk about the physics and engineering involved in making the marble run and in how the marble moves.

2. Give each student an equal amount of foam track pieces. I usually give them two 6" split pieces and one 6" tube each. If they want smaller lengths, I cut them from their 6" pieces.

3. Share rolls of tape between 2 or 3 people.

4. You can work with a partner or in teams to create larger runs.

5. Give them each a marble and watch them go.

The lesson:

The marble has potential energy that is ready to be released when it is at the top of the run. That energy turns into kinetic energy (motion) when it rolls down the hill. Gravity determines the speed of marble motion; steeper angles make faster runs.

Vocabulary: energy, potential energy, kinetic energy, gravity, angles

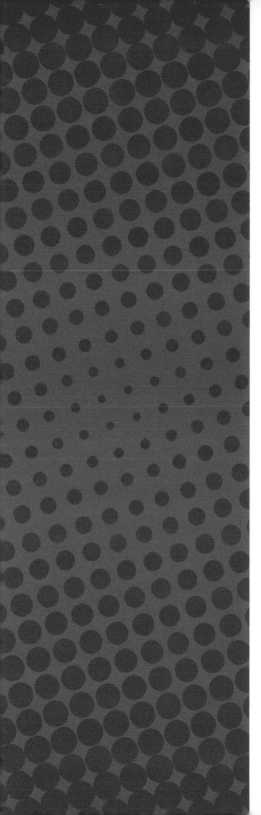

Water Runs

Many of us delight in creating streams, dams and simply playing with water.

Creating streams, diversions and gullies with water is many people's version of a perfect activity. With this activity students control the flow of water and engineer it to go where they want. It is described here using a wading pool and pipe insulators but you can create the same thing with a hose on trickle and a mud or sand slope.

Materials:

- Small wading pool
- Water thermos spigot
- Two 2" × 2" pieces of 1/16"-1/8 rubber to act as a gasket between the spigot fitting and pool
- Caulking or strong waterproof adhesive
- Pipe insulation foam or PVC pipe cut lengthwise
- Masking tape

How to:

1. Cut a hole to fit the thermos spigot fitting in the side of the wading pool (at the lowest point you can).

2. Cut the same size hole in the gasket material and adhere one inside and one outside the pool sides. Let the adhesive dry.

3. Install the spigot in the hole.

4. Now you can put the pool on a table or elevated surface, fill it with water and children can just press the button when they want water to flow out.

5. Tape insulation or pipes to the spigot and to each other to get water to flow wherever you want it.

How to present it to your group:

1. Talk about water engineering, canals, dams and water conservation. Also talk about fun.

2. Divide up the pipes, tools and tape so the canal building is a team effort.

3. You can give students a challenge to move the water to a certain place or just let them invent their own engineering projects.

The lesson:

Diverting and moving water is a great introduction to the physics of motion, energy and gravity as well as a lesson in careful engineering. Students learn that gravity is important to the speed and flow of water. Engineering and building play a key role in creating a project that functions and contains the water.

Vocabulary:

Gravity, dams, water flow, motion, energy

Race Track Physics

Children enjoy rolling things down a track and are more than willing to drop things if you ask them to.

This activity is an exciting way to demonstrate the physics of friction and falling objects and to race some cool things. I started doing this experiment to demonstrate the simple physics principle that 2 objects of different weight and mass will fall at the same rate if dropped through the air. When you take the same two objects and roll them down a hill or track, the heavier object will go faster.

Materials:

- Smooth track that can be angled and hold two objects: Hot Wheels track, Blu-Track or even cardboard sheets
- Small cars of different weight
- Small balls of assorted sizes
- Tape
- Paper, pencil and clipboard to record results

How to:

1. Set your tracks up so 2 objects can race side by side at the same angle. Use tape to secure it for multiple use.

2. Divide the cars into "light" cars and "heavy" cars. Do the same for the balls.

3. Race a "light" car against a "heavy" car at least 3 times on the track and record the result. Take the same two cars and drop them from an equal height and record which lands first on your chart. Summarize.

4. Try the same thing with the balls.

How to present it to your group:

1. Explain the principles first and then conduct experiments to see if they are true.

2. Have several sets of cars, balls and at least 2 track sets.

3. Have teams of students so that everyone is involved. Take turns with cars and balls as well as switching sets once they have recorded their data.

4. Consider having an adult do the charting.

5. Once students have seen the data recorded and understand the experiment, let them free play with the tracks. They will continue learning on their own.

The lesson:

This is a physics lesson that demonstrates the principles of gravity, energy and resistance. Two objects will fall (gravity) at the same rate of speed if you drop them through the air. If you roll them down a track they will travel at different rates because of resistance (where and how the object touches the surface of the track).

Preschool version:

The first part of this experiment for preschoolers is to gather them and explain how gravity and friction affect the speed of dropping objects and rolling objects. The students will generally let you demonstrate dropping balls and rolling cars once before they get restless. Try to wrap this up in 5 minutes.

Set the tracks up and an area for ball dropping. Have children cycle through the stations, experimenting and taking turns with both processes. Older children may continuously roll cars down the track while your youngest students may just observe. If they are engaged in some way, it is appropriate for their stage of development. The activity will usually hold attention for 10-15 minutes.

Vocabulary:

Physics, friction, resistance energy, motion

CHAPTER 6

EDIBLE SCIENCE AND ART

Sculpt a Chocolate Pastry

Sculpt, bake and eat your own delicious pastry using packaged crescent dough and chocolate chips. The art in this project is the sculpting of the dough, the science is observing how heat changes the form of the chocolate and the dough. Eating the project is a tasty bonus.

Materials:

- Pre-made grocery store crescent dough (the kind that comes in a tube)
- Chocolate chips
- Flat baking pans and access to an oven.
- Paper and pen for making a chart

How to:

1. Take a triangle of pre-cut crescent dough and wrap chocolate chips inside or outside it.

2. Sculpt it into any shape.

3. Put it on a pan and bake according to package instructions.

How to have your group make it:

1. Put a paper towel or plate at each seat.

2. Put 8 chocolate chips on each towel or plate.

3. Have students wash or sanitize their hands and sit in their seat – no touching the chips!

4. Explain that this cooking project is an art and science project that will be good to eat. The science is what the heat does to the hard chocolate

(melts it) and the dough (evaporates moisture and allows it to rise). The art is in sculpting the dough into different shapes.

5. Demonstrate wrapping 5-6 chocolate chips into a crescent shape. I then tell the students that because I am an artist I like to take it to another level and make interesting shapes. I demonstrate an elephant, an owl, a slug and finally, a ball with eyes.

6. Show the students how you place the shape on the pan and then use the paper and pen to make a chart showing whose pastry is whose. This is necessary because the heat of the oven will change the shape of the dough and this allows us to identify individual pastries.

7. Give each student a triangle of dough. Remind them not to knead (push in) the dough on their paper towel as it will stick. Urge them to make their creation in a timely manner as the dough will soften fast in their warm (but clean) hands.

8. Have students bring the pastry to you at the pan so you can write their name on the chart in the position that corresponds with their pastry on the pan.

9. Put the pan in the oven and bake according to instructions.

10. When the pastry is done, let them cool and pass them out. Do not eat until everyone has been served!

Other things you can do with this project:

1. You can make savory (not sweet) pastries by using cheese and lunchmeat, we have used turkey, ham and salami. You can also make "pizza pockets" by using pizza sauce, cheese and pepperoni.

The lesson:

This experiment integrates both science and art. The application of heat energy (from the oven) causes chocolate to melt into a liquid form much like heat melts ice. The chocolate molecules are still chocolate but they take a different form because of their temperature. Temperature also affects the pastry dough, causing it to rise and change form. The sculpting of the raw dough and chocolate is the art piece of this project.

Preschool version:

The first part of our edible science/art activity is sculpting the chocolate and dough. We do a secondary activity like block play indoors or game playing outdoors while we wait for our food to cook. As we eat the delicious pastry we talk about taste and heat and how fun it is to eat!

Cupcake Science and Art

Mixing batter has all the elements of a good scientific potion; measurements, combination of ingredients, etc. The finishing touch of decorating with sticks and a palette of colored frosting results in varied artistic masterpieces. The eating of the cupcake is a satisfying end to a project well done.

Materials:

- Boxed yellow cake mix -
- Eggs-
- Vegetable oil-
- Water-

- White frosting-
- Chocolate frosting-
- Food coloring-

- Mixing bowl-
- Mixing spoon-
- Two cup measuring pitcher-

- Cupcake pans-
- Cupcake papers-
- Popsicle sticks-

How to present it to your group:

Have groups of 3-6 children mix their own batch of batter. This turns into 4 or 5 cupcakes per child so I only do it when we have a specific baking or cooking class. Each member of the group should be responsible for one job plus mixing. There are 3 eggs to be cracked, 1 amount of water to be measured and poured, 1 measure of oil to be poured and 1 bag of dry mix to be added. Everybody takes even turns mixing and filling the cupcake papers.

Our normal routine is to make one batch for every 20 students. In this case I will have the students gather and I add the ingredients. I ask them to help by closing my eyes when I pour the water and oil; letting them tell me when it is at the proper measure. I often juggle eggs and do egg toss with my assistants for a bit of dramatic flair. I then have everyone stir 5 times while I hold the bowl. I put the batter in the cupcake papers in the pans and put them in the oven.

Once the cupcakes are cooled we can begin the artistic part of decorating:

1. Use white frosting and food coloring to create several colors of frosting; don't forget the chocolate. Make color palettes on paper plates so that generous dollops of each color are on as many plates as you need for the class. I will often have a separate plate for chocolate and white frosting. Put popsicle sticks in each color as spreaders.

2. You can also put frosting in plastic sandwich bags, twist tie the opening, trim the corner with scissors and you have an instant piping bag.

3. Wash hands and explain the hygiene of not licking spreading sticks, fingers or in-process cupcakes. Etiquette requires that nobody eats until all are done or it is allowed by the instructor.

4. Make a demonstration cupcake design so they see how to use the popsicle sticks as spreaders and frosting brushes. If you are using piping bags, show them how to use those for detail.

5. Pass the cupcakes out and have fun.

The lesson:

The science is in the mixing and measuring of ingredients and the application of heat (baking). Decorating with different colored frosting adds an art element to the project.

Preschool version:

There are four parts to our cupcake making; the first is the measuring, mixing and baking of ingredients (very scientific). The second step is the oven baking time, third is decorating with frosting (art), the last is eating (the reward for a successful project). Each of these steps takes 10-15 minutes and timing is important.

It is important that the children are present during measuring and mixing but need to be engaged with something else during oven time. The cupcakes should cool completely before decorating so there is at least 30 minutes between coming out of the oven and spreading frosting. Finally, you want to think about when you want your children to eat a cupcake. I usually have them eat just before pick-up!

• •

Dancing Raisins

When you say, "we are going to watch raisins dance" children are curious. When you tell them that the fizzy bubbles in ginger ale are the raisins "partner" in the dance, they really want to see it. This is a great observing, waiting and then seeing project. Children's eyes are glued to their cup of raisins and ginger ale. Some dance a lot, some dance a little and occasionally, some don't dance at all. At the end of the dance, ups and downs are forgotten when the children are given the choice to eat their raisins and drink their ginger ale.

Materials:

- Ginger Ale
- Raisins: 3 or 4 per cup
- A 9-ounce transparent plastic cup

How to present it to your group:

1. Put a cup that is 3/4 filled with ginger ale in front of each student

2. Explain that the bubbles in the ginger ale are going to be attracted to the raisins. They will attach themselves to the nooks and crannies in the raisin, dance to the surface with it, pop at the top, then the raisin will slowly dance back down to the bottom of the cup until it dances up again.

3. Allow plenty of time for observations and exclamations.

4. When the dance is over, allow students to eat their raisins and/or drink the ginger ale.

The lesson:

The raisins are denser than the liquid and sink to the bottom of the cup at first. The carbon dioxide bubbles in the ginger ale attach themselves to the crevices on the raisin, lifting the raisin up, then popping and lowering the raisin: up, down, up, down; like a dance!

Fruit and Vegetable Engineering

Students can create elaborate structures that really hold together using grapes, carrots and celery. The bonus is eating the joints and fittings when the project is done.

Materials:

Fruit and Vegetables: you can use several items for construction or just one. I base my materials on the time of year and what is on sale at the market.

- Grapes
- Diced or sliced carrot pieces
- Diced or sliced celery pieces
- Round toothpicks
- 8"-10" paper plates

How to present it to your group:

1. Thoroughly wash all fruit and vegetables.

2. Dice and/or slice vegetables into 1/4"-1/2" pieces.

3. Have all engineers, architects and construction workers thoroughly wash their hands.

4. Put plates with toothpicks, fruit and vegetables in front of each student.

5. Replenish supplies and encourage elaborate structures.

The lesson:

If this activity had a technology component (motorized appendages?) it would encompass all the S.T.E.A.M.—science, technology, engineering, art and math criteria. Some students will cover science by constructing what look like DNA strands. We talk about engineering stronger structures by comparing the strength of triangular supports to cubes. Artists among us build beautiful structures and mathematicians make a variety of geometric shapes.

Lifesaver Taste Test

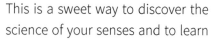

This is a sweet way to discover the science of your senses and to learn how a "blind" taste test works. It is also a thrill to go to "candy school" and memorize the colors and flavors of the Lifesaver hard candies. This is like controlled lab tests except that we only get data once instead of multiple times (too many candies).

Materials:

- Lifesaver hard candies in 5 fruit flavors

How to present it to your group:

1. Explain that scientists start with a theory (idea) and then conduct tests/experiments to see if the idea is true.

2. Your theory is that although you use your tongue to taste things, it is your nose that does most of the detecting of flavors.

3. The idea (hypothesis) is that your tongue can only sense sweet, salty, sour and bitter flavors. It is your tongue that tastes more variety of flavors like fruits, chocolate and other flavors. You are going to test this idea by doing "blind" tests of Lifesaver candy.

4. Conduct "candy school" by telling them that they must first memorize the five flavors and colors of the candy. My students are always very attentive at this point. I hold each color and tell them the flavor and then we repeat with them telling me the flavor. Everyone is focused on passing with flying colors.

5. Assign groups of two (usually those sitting together). Tell them that one is going to be the "taster" first while the other is the "feeder," then they will switch roles. Assure them that each will get a chance at both roles and see if they can come to an agreement as to who goes first.

6. Have the "taster" close their eyes so they don't see the lifesaver color. They will then pinch their nose so they are only sensing through their mouth.

7. Have the "feeder" gently put the lifesaver on the front of the "tasters" tongue. Once the lifesaver color is hidden in their mouth, the "taster" can open their eyes but keep holding their nose.

8. Ask the questions: What do you taste? Do you taste any flavor? Do you taste sweet, salty, bitter, sour?

9. After the questions are asked the students let go of their nose and sense the difference in their ability to taste. Do they taste more flavor now?

10. Some students will see this as a guessing contest. Remind them that it is the taste experience that counts and not guessing the flavor "right." Remind others not to give away the candy colors and flavors to the "tasters."

11. Be sure that everyone gets a chance to be a "taster" and a "feeder."

12. Students can eat the candy or spit it out into the trash.

The lesson:

This activity uses a blind taste test to illustrate the importance of recording data (in the form of responses) and making a statistical analysis by comparing multiple results. A show of hands gives a small statistical snapshot but the children should be aware of the need for hundreds of results to get a meaningful conclusion.

Marshmallow Geometry

How many geometric shapes can you build? Does the geometry change when you eat them? This delicious project combines, building, engineering and math. Children build geometric shapes using toothpicks and mini-marshmallows. You can build everything from triangles and squares to octahedrons, icosahedrons and many more. It's fun, easy and sweet.

Materials:

- Mini marshmallows
- Round toothpicks
- Paper plates
- Printed examples of geometric shapes

How to present it to your group:

1. Make a sample of a simple shape and a more complex shape. I usually start with a triangle, a pyramid and a cube.

2. Show students your samples and show them how you put the toothpicks in the marshmallows to form shapes. Let them know that they will get as much material as they need to create their geometric shapes.

3. Show them the chart of geometric shapes that you printed from the internet or a book. Read some of the geometric names and speculate about interesting shapes.

4. Be specific about how many marshmallows they can eat now and how much they keep intact for later.

5. Put the shape charts where children can see them.

6. Put an 8"-10" paper plate at each student's place. They will build right on the plate.

7. Put marshmallows and toothpicks on student plates.

8. Replenish marshmallows and toothpicks as necessary. You will go through toothpicks faster than marshmallows.

The lesson:

Children will be hands-on in creating geometric shapes. Shapes and angles will not be an abstract concept when students make their own. You will see everything from one dimensional squares and triangles to complex three dimensional, multi-sided shapes.

 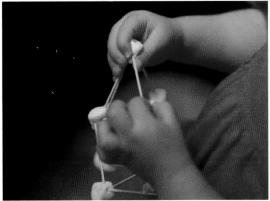

Preschool version:

Squares, cubes, triangles and pyramids are simple shapes that children can build to understand a bit about shapes and building. Use simple shapes and geometry and building vocabulary. This is a fun activity that generally lasts 15-20 minutes.

Vocabulary:

Geometry, geometric, strut, support, cube, three dimensional, one dimensional

Personal Pizza

"Pizza Wednesday" is always one of the most popular cooking activities in our Summer camp programs. Each student creates his or her own pizza the way they want it. I use cheese and pepperoni as toppings but you could add anything you liked. The children enjoy this project thoroughly and often repeat it at home.

Materials:

1. English muffin half
2. Pepperoni: sliced, diced or mini rounds
3. Cheese: grated
4. Bottled pizza sauce: I like the squeeze bottle
5. Baking pan
6. Access to an oven

How to present it to your group:

1. Preheat oven to 400 F.

2. Cut English muffins in half.

3. Put grated cheese and cut-up pepperoni on several plates.

4. Have everyone wash their hands.

5. Demonstrate the making of a pizza by putting sauce on an English muffin, putting some cheese on and then artistically (portrait, landscape, face?) putting pepperoni on.

6. Explain that when they complete the pizza they should bring it to you at the pan and make sure that you put their name on the chart where it corresponds to the location of their pizza on the pan.

7. Talk about avoiding the spread of germs during communal cooking. No licking fingers without washing hands again, no grabbing bits of cheese and putting food and fingers in mouth. No licking spoons or forks.

8. Put a plate or paper towel in front of each student.

9. Put the paper plates with cheese and pepperoni in the center of tables so everyone can reach them.

10. Give each student an English muffin half.

11. Go around the table and give each student that wants one (some children do not want sauce) a "splort" of sauce. Have someone following behind you spreading the sauce.

12. Once their "splort" of sauce is spread, students can add whatever ingredients they want. Be aware that some students may not want sauce.

13. Put the full pans in the oven for 10-12 minutes.

The lesson:

The children can be artistically creative in arranging the pepperoni and/or cheese on the pizza. I usually make a sample pizza that has a pepperoni smiley face. Applying heat to cheese changes the way the cheese molecules act (they melt); this is a good question to ask, as well as why heat makes the English muffin crust "crispy."

Rainbow Cakes

This is a delicious way to play around with the science of mixing and baking a small loaf cake. The layering of colored batter adds to the potion making and gives the final baked cake an artistic surprise. You can combine this with decorating the cake to add even more art dimension.

Materials:

- 1 Boxed cake mix
- 4 six inch by three inch loaf pans (foil pans are fine)
- 3 eggs
- ½ cup oil
- One cup water
- Food coloring
- One big mixing bowl and 3 or 4 small ones
- Mixing spoons

How to present it to your group:

You can mix the whole batch in one big bowl and pour the batter into 3 or 4 small bowls to be colored or: Break into three groups/tables, measure the ingredients equally into the small mixing bowl at each table (i.e. one egg, 1/3 dry mix, 1/3 cup water, 1/6 cup oil for each). Have each table create a different color batter mix.

For this version I am going to describe mixing in one big bowl and coloring in the small bowls.

1. Explain the entire process and what we hope to get from it.

2. Have the students break into 3 or 4 color mixing groups. Give each one a small mixing bowl.

3. Put the ingredients in the mixing bowl according to the box recipe – explaining what each ingredient is going to add to the whole.

4. Have each student participate in stirring the mix. I usually go around the class holding the bowl and having each person stir 5 times.

5. Pour the well mixed batter equally into the small mixing bowl at each group's station

6. Have each group pick a color as you go around adding the appropriate food coloring.

7. Have the group mix it up and bring it to you at the loaf pans.

8. Add a small layer of each color to each pan. Layer color on top of color.

9. Put it in the oven as per box instructions.

The lesson:

The science is in the combining and mixing of ingredients, the layering of colored batter in cake pans and the application of heat to create risen cakes. The art is in how the colors are layered and the beauty of the finished cake.

Preschool version:

If you have an adult for each 3-6 students you can mix the batter ingredients at each table. Otherwise, mix the batter ingredients in front of the class, allowing each person to mix it five times. Pour some batter into a bowl at each table, have each table dye the batter a different color. I like to handle the food coloring but the children can mix the color and batter together. Layer the different colored batter in pans as described above and put the pans in the oven. This part of the process will have taken around 20-30 minutes; the children will be ready to get up and do something active while the cakes are baking.

When the cakes have cooled, gather everyone to marvel at the rainbow colored inside of the cake and enjoy a delicious slice.

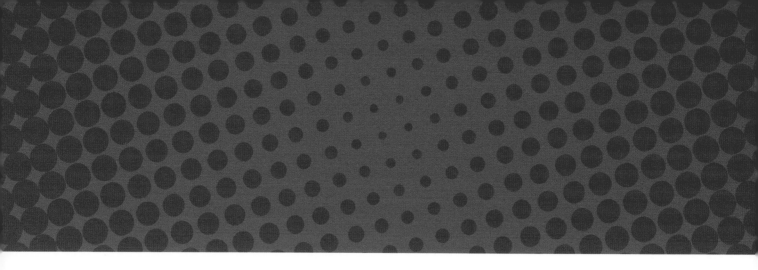

Savory Pocket Pastry

Children can learn to make their own delicious savory hand-held pastry with this activity whose science is like chocolate pastry sculpture but the result is quite different. It makes for a much heartier snack and the children are pleased that they made a substantial meal item.

Materials:

- A rectangle of supermarket crescent dough (2 triangles crimped together)
- Lunchmeat: Ham, Turkey, Salami, etc. (or cooked vegetables)
- Cheese
- Access to an oven
- Baking pan
- Paper to identify pastry

How to present it to your group:

Preheat oven to 375

1. Put plates or napkins at each student's place.

2. Dice the lunchmeat and/or vegetables, grate the cheese and put it on plates accessible to the students.

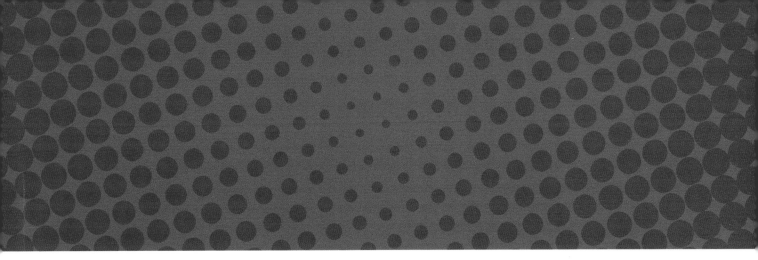

3. Be sure to have crimped the score between the triangles on the rectangle of dough so it holds together.

4. Demonstrate to students how to lay the rectangle down, fill it with the ingredients of their choice, fold the sides and the ends and crimp them together.

5. Lay the pastry pockets on the pan and be sure to use your paper to identify whose is which.

6. Bake at 375 for 10-15 minutes.

The lesson:

The application of heat energy (from the oven) causes cheese to melt much like heat melts ice. The cheese molecules are still cheese but they take a different form because of the temperature. Temperature also affects the pastry dough, causing it to rise and change form.

CHAPTER 7

MOSAIC GLASS ART PROJECTS

Mosaic Coaster or Trivet/Hot Pad

Mosaic coasters and trivets make wonderful and beautiful practical art pieces for the dining table or in the kitchen. This is a quick, fun and easy lesson that yields beautiful works of art. I have done thousands of these with students for Mother's Day, Father's Day and gift-giving projects.

Materials:

- 6" wall tile for trivet, 4" wall tile for coaster
- Tumbled stained glass or flat items like coins, beach glass, wood or pebbles
- Felt squares (just smaller than the tile) or stick-on cork or felt pads (1/2" or bigger) for the back of the tile
- Elmer's Glue-All (white glue) or Weldbond Glue

How to present it to your group:

1. Put glass or other material in trays or bins around the classroom so students can access them.

2. Give each student a tile. With Pre-K through second grade I take care of the backing by gluing a felt square to the bottom of the tile or affixing the cork or felt stick-on dots. With 3rd grade and above I have the students perform that task.

3. I like to put the glass in containers around the room and allow students to get up and find just the right pieces for their design. I give them a small collecting plate and they can "treasure hunt" multiple times. This allows the tactile artists and people who are restless to enjoy the project by moving around. The tactile part of the process brings joy to many students who otherwise hurry through art projects.

4. Emphasize to students that anything they can draw or paint, they can create with the mosaic material. The material is also beautiful in abstract designs, patterns and colors on their tile. If they are trying to create a picture of something like a flower, they should make sure that the background color contrasts (is different than) the color of the main image. The mosaic tile work is like creating an art puzzle. Many students take great delight in carefully piecing the shapes together. There is no wrong way to do the creative part of the project.

5. Curb your expectations. Most Pre-K to 2nd grade students will do abstract designs with colors and shapes. It is only when students are older that they can do a lot of representational art. I never bring samples to class because I don't want a Kindergarten student trying to do the work of a ten-year-old. It only frustrates the child and turns them off the subject.

6. Spread glue evenly on the tile using the tip of the glue bottle. It should be spread thick enough to hold the glass but not so thick that it runs and drips on the table. The glue will dry clear so don't worry too much. It is often easiest with younger students to have an adult spreading glue on the tiles while the children are collecting glass pieces. Older students will have their own glue techniques.

7. Once the student is finished with the tile, put it on a drying table. You can write the students' names on a piece of masking tape and put it on the top of the tile or you could have them put their names on the bottom before they start using the glue and glass. Elmer's Glue-All and Weldbond take one to two hours to dry at room temperature.

Preschool version:

Younger children are fascinated with the glass but have a shorter attention span for sitting down and creating than the older children do. Put the tile in front of each child and have an adult apply glue to the whole tile. Skip the walking around and collecting part of the lesson and put plates/bins of mixed glass in the middle of the table in front of groups of children and let them search through the bins. They will then put their selections directly on the tile. Expect the explanation and project to last 25-40 minutes. Some children will finish sooner than others and should be allowed free play (after washing up).

Mosaic Stepping Stone – Direct to wet cement

This is a wonderful way to make mosaic stepping stones quickly in just one class session using the direct inlay method. With this method you mix "sand mix" cement in a wheelbarrow or mixing trough, pour it into plant saucers or any plastic (or cardboard) containers deeper than 1". You can use anything you like as the mosaic material. I like to use tumbled (no sharp edges) stained glass but you can use tiles, beach glass, coins, keys, rocks, beads, shells and many other things. The cement takes two days to set up but you can send your students home the same day as the project and they can wait to take it out of the mold at home.

Materials:

- "Sand Mix" (sand and cement) or "Mortar Mix" (stickier sand and cement) pre-mixed bags from the hardware store.

- A wheelbarrow or mixing trough for mixing the cement mix and water.

- A hoe or shovel for mixing

- Gloves

- Plastic plant saucers, pie tins or cardboard box bottoms sprayed with cooking oil or anything that is 8" wide and at least 1" deep that you can use as a mold

- Beautiful things to put on the cement. Preferably beach glass or tumbled stained glass

How to:

1. Lay the tumbled glass or other material out in trays or plates so that participants can collect what they want using small plates or cups.

2. Lay your design out on a paper template or on your working surface before you get your mold filled with cement. This way you know what your design looks like and you can easily get it on the wet cement.

3. When you have your material and your design ready, take your mold and have it filled with cement. Place your pieces into the wet cement. If a glass piece is flat, you must tap it down until it is flush (flat) to the surface of the cement. It is important that the glass be flush with no edges showing. Glass chunks, shells and rocks should be submerged a little more than halfway into the cement.

4. Sometimes water rises over your glass pieces making you think they are sinking. They are not sinking! They are just being covered up by the water separating from the cement and rising.

5. Tomorrow you can rub the top of your stone with a damp cloth or brush to remove dusty, crusty cement residue from the glass surface. Pieces that you thought were submerged will triumphantly appear at this point.

6. Keep your stone and mold in the shade and out of the rain for 2 days. After 2 days you can release it from the mold by turning it over and flexing the sides of the mold.

Mixing Cement

1. We recommend that you use a pre-mixed "topping mix," "sand mix" or "mortar mix." Do not use the pre-mixes that have rocks in them. Mixing instructions are on the bag but you can be successful by adding one gallon of water to 60 pounds of mix. You can put in a little extra water if the weather is warm or your mixing box absorbs water. You can use an electric mixer or just mix it in a wheelbarrow with a hoe or shovel.

2. Fill the molds to about 1/4"-1/8" from the top. Make sure the surface is flat and smooth. Fill molds on demand, do not try to fill too many ahead of time as the water will begin separating from the mix and become too wet to inlay flat things.

Preschool version:

Put bins of glass in the center of the table in front of groups of children. Have them pick out 20 pieces of glass to start as you are filling molds with cement. The tapping of the glass pieces is the most essential step and most children will need help with that. Have an adult go over the stepping stones after the children are done to make sure pieces are tapped flat into wet cement.

CHAPTER 8

PHYSICAL GROUP GAMES

Mr. or Mrs. Clock: "What Time Is It?"

This is a gentle tag game that allows everyone to participate at their own pace. The action is well supervised and there are a couple of strategies for winning. This is a great "starter game" that does not alienate anyone or get rough, especially if it is well supervised.

To start:

Pick a person to be Mr. or Mrs. Clock. Have them stand behind a line or against a tree or wall; this is their base. Have the rest of the group stand facing them, 25-40 feet away, behind a line or against a wall or tree; this is their base.

The object:

You can win (and become the Clock) by being the first to tag the Clock or the last person not to be tagged by the Clock and his/her helpers.

To play:

The group will say to the Clock in unison: "Mr./Mrs. Clock, Mr./Mrs. Clock, what time is it?" The Clock will reply with a number between 1 and 12. Each player will take that many steps toward the Clock. Long steppers are hoping to tag the Clock, short steppers are hoping to be the last one not to be tagged (remember, there are two strategies to win). It is important for the game supervisor to make sure the steps are correct; the temptation to skip, jump or miscount exists.

As the steppers get closer, the Clock has the option to respond "midnight!" to the time question and then chase and tag steppers. Anyone tagged before they get back to the base becomes the Clock's helper in tagging people. The call, answer, stepping and tagging continues until the Clock is tagged or only one person is left as a stepper.

Food Tag

The theme of this game is a subject that everyone understands and it allows players freedom to determine the direction they want to run (there are four bases to go to). Players never feel trapped because their decision to run is based on their own "taste."

To start:

You will need to make four paper signs. The first sign is a smiling face for "like," the second is a heart for "love," the third is a frowning face for "dislike" and the fourth is a question mark "?" for "I do not know." Put these signs up equidistant from each other in four corners of the play space. A space of 20-30 feet apart is good, but you can vary it if you need to. These signs are safe base.

Pick one person to be the first food caller; that person stands at the center of the area. The other players start at any base of their choice.

The object:

The winner is the last person to remain untagged.

To play:

The food caller starts at the center, while the other players start at any base. The caller shouts out a food like "steamed broccoli." The players run to the appropriate base according to their opinion of the food: like, love, dislike, don't know. The caller tries to tag them as they run; if they are caught, they become helpers and join the food caller to consult on the next food called. Only the original food caller's voice should shout out foods. The game supervisor should stand with the caller to keep the game moving swiftly and to edit the food choices as needed.

Capture the Flag

This is a strategic tag game that pits one team against the other in a quest to capture the other team's flag and cross the centerline with it. It can be played in an open field or yard as well as in more complex places like small forests and parks. When the boundaries are well defined and understood by all players, varied types of spaces will work. It is important to explain the strategies, rules and boundaries carefully so that everyone understands them.

To start:

You will need to make two distinctly different but equal flags; tape and paper on a stick will work just fine. Make a center line that equally divides the playing field. One side of this line will be a safe zone for team 1 and the other side for team 2. Create a space toward the back of each safe zone for placing the flag and draw a circle 5-10 feet around the flag; guards are not allowed in this zone unless they have chased an opponent in to it. Create a jail base 20-30 feet from the flag and draw a circle 5-10 feet around this jail base; guards are not allowed in this zone unless they are in hot pursuit of an opponent.

Divide your group into two equal teams. Each team should be identified by bandanas, armbands or clearly visible tape. I often use two colors of duct tape to identify teams. Lead both groups around to understand what the object of the game is and where the dividing line, the flags, the jails and the boundary lines are.

The object:

To score a point, a player from team 1 must capture the flag of team 2 and cross the dividing line into their own territory with the flag, without getting tagged. The flag is returned after each point is scored. If we are playing in a forest or large area, we will switch sides after each point.

To play:

Start by having players line up on their side of the dividing line facing their opponents. They will see who is on their team and who is on the other. The game supervisor will start counting backwards from ten; during the count, the teams can take up positions wherever they want on their side of the line. Some will play defense (near the flag), while others will get ready to go on offense. At the end of the count, game supervisor will shout *"Game on!"* And players can go wherever they want.

If a player is tagged while in the other team's territory, they go to that team's jail base. The only way to get out of jail is if your own teammate sneaks across the line and tags you in jail. You both then get a safe, free walk back (linking arms or holding hands). The game supervisor has the option to yell *"Jail break"* in which case all players in all jails get a free walk back to their safe side.

If a player is tagged in the other team's territory while carrying the flag, they go to jail and the flag is returned to its original spot.

The flag should always be displayed in the same spot in plain sight. Hiding the flag adds a level of difficulty and frustration that causes arguments and delays.

Poison Dart Frog

This is a fun and dramatic game of observation that is best played with groups of 6-15 players. It requires an involved game supervisor and the cooperation of each player to stick by the rules.

To start:

Have your group sit in a circle on the ground so that everyone can see each other. There should be 6-12" of space between each seated player.

The object:

One player will be the poison dart frog who will eliminate his/her victims (other players) by sticking his/her tongue out at them. Another player is the detective trying to figure out who the poison dart frog is. The detective can win by correctly guessing who the frog is. The dart frog wins if the detective makes two incorrect guesses or if the dart frog eliminates all players before being identified.

To play:

Explain the game: One person will be the poison dart frog trying to eliminate people by quickly sticking his/her tongue out at them without being seen by the detective. It is important that players constantly look around the circle so they know when the frog is sticking a tongue out at them. It is equally important that they "die" (lay down with a gasp or dramatic flair) when the frog eliminates them. Do not give away the frog's identity and make sure to stay in a position so everyone knows you are eliminated.

The detective has two chances to guess who the frog is. When they have a suspect, they must tell the game supervisor they are making an official guess. If the detective guesses correctly within two tries or guesses incorrectly twice, the game ends and a new frog and detective are picked. The game also ends if the frog eliminates everybody.

Start by having everyone in the circle close their eyes so the game supervisor can pick the frog and the detective. The supervisor walks around the circle letting everyone know that the frog will be picked by giving two pats on that person's head, and the detective will be picked with one tap on the head. Walking around the circle several times (talking to distract) as you pick the frog and detective is an effective way to keep other players from noticing who you tap.

Have everyone open their eyes and ask the detective to sit in the center of the circle. The game begins.

Sponge Water Relay

This is a fun and spirited relay game played outdoors when it is warm enough to occasionally get splashed with water. You will need 3-4 sponges of equal size and an equal number of 1-2-quart plastic bottles with a wide opening. The opening of the bottles should be small enough to make it challenging to squeeze water from a sponge into it but not so small that it creates frustration. You will also need a bucket or buckets holding 5-6 gallons of water.

Another variation of this game is to use ladles instead of sponges to relay the water.

To start:
With a pen or tape, create a level line toward the top of each bottle. This is the amount of water they need to fill to finish. Divide your group into equal teams of 4-5 people, and give each team a sponge and a bottle. I like to have chairs as raised platforms for the bottle. This makes it less likely to accidently spill. Fill buckets with water and put them 30-60 feet away from each team's bottle and sponge (equidistant).

To play:
Each team forms a line behind their bucket. The player in front runs the sponge to the buckets of water, runs them back, squeezes water into the bottle and then hands the sponge to the next person in line and goes to the back of the line. The bottle must stay on the platform (no holding it). You cannot pour spilled water into your bottle. The relay continues until the bottle is filled to the finish line.

The object:
Your team can finish by filling the bottle to the finish line. We don't end the game until all bottles are filled to the line. This allows all teams to finish; we sometimes have teams who finish early and get in line to help the other teams. You can play the whole relay as a cooperative relay this way if you choose.

Kick the Can

This is a classic outdoor game that has elements of hide and seek, capture the flag and tag. All you need to play is an outdoor space with spots for hiding and a can or bottle. A plastic bottle or can will work much better than metal. If you want it to make some noise when you kick it (as a metal one would), then put some pebbles in it.

To start:

Create boundaries for the game and emphasize that everyone must stay inside the boundary. Place the can in the center of the play area. Create a "jail" space about 20 feet or more away from the can area.

To play:

Designate someone as being "it." This person stands at the can, closes and covers their eyes and counts to 30. While he/she is counting, the other players must hide within the boundary. When the count is done, the person who is "it" looks for other players. When they spot another player, they shout out the players name; that is, "I see Gus!" and run to kick the can before "Gus" does. If "Gus" reaches the can and kicks it before the "it" person then "Gus" is free to hide again while "it" counts to 30.

If a player who is not spotted can get to the can and kick it before the "it" person spots them, then all players are free from "jail" and the "it" person counts again. The game supervisor has the option to start a new game with a new "it" person at any time.

The object:

The game is over when all players are in "jail" or if the last person hiding can kick the can before the "it" person.

Sharks and Minnows

You can enjoy several variations of this simple tag game. The idea of being a shark or running from sharks is thrilling to most of us.

To start:

Create a boundary with a "safe base" line on opposite sides. This can be on a playground, in a field or even in a pool. Designate one or two people as "sharks" and make them stand in the middle of the playing area. The rest of the group stands behind one of the baselines.

To play:

The "sharks" yell out "cross the ocean" or something similar; players (minnows) run across the field to the opposite side. If a shark tags a minnow, that minnow becomes a shark. **Variation:** When a shark tags a minnow, he/she becomes "seaweed" and must stand where tagged. The "seaweed" can tag runners who then become "seaweed."

The object:

The round is over if all players have been tagged to become sharks or seaweed, or if the last runner makes it through the ocean untagged.

Freeze Tag

Freeze tag allows you to take a simple tag game and add an "unfreezing" component that touches on physical and mental developmental stages. In this version, children must pass between a "frozen" person's legs to free him/her. The players practice coordination, agility, compassion, strategy and timing, all while getting exercise and having fun.

To start:

You need a good-sized running space with a safe base line on either end. Freeze tag is best played with groups of eight or more but you can manage with any number by adjusting the size of the playing field and/or the number of taggers.

To play:

Designate the boundaries and safe base lines. Pick one person to be the tagger; if your group size or temperament warrants it, pick two taggers. Players run across the play field from one base to the other, trying to avoid getting tagged. When they are tagged, they must "freeze" in place until another runner frees them by crawling through their legs.

The object:

The game finishes when all runners have been "frozen" or when there is only one runner left.

Blob Tag

Blob tag emphasizes teamwork, cooperation and makes students aware of spatial relationships. It is also a tremendous amount of fun!

To start:

Designate a playing field with boundaries and have children spread out around the playing field. There are no bases. Assign two players to start the blob after the players have spread out on the field.

To play:

The first two members of the blob hold hands or link elbows and then try to tag other players with their free hand/hands without letting go of the other player in their blob. When a player gets tagged, they join the blob on one of the ends. Only the outside hands of the blob can tag players. The blob must be linked when tagging; if the link breaks, the tag is invalid. When the blob reaches four players, the blob separates into two blobs. Blobs do not tag each other. Another variation is to have one giant blob, but this increases the likelihood of falling and makes tagging far more challenging.

The object:

The game is over when everyone has become part of a blob.

Red Light, Green Light

A great game for developing listening, observation and agility skills in all players, including the one who is the traffic light. The game is appropriate for all ages but especially popular with groups of young children.

To start:

Designate a playing field with a start line on one end, a finish line about 3/4 of the way down the field and a place for the "traffic light" to stand: 5-10 feet beyond the finish line. Assign one player to be the traffic light. Have the "traffic light" stand beyond the finish line while the rest of the players stand on the start line.

To play:

The "traffic light" turns his/her back to the other players and says, "Green light." The other players move (walk) toward the finish line. At any time, the "light" can say, "Red light" and then turn toward the others (they must speak first and turn second). The moving players must stop moving forward when they hear "red light." If the "light" catches them moving, they must go back to the start line. It is important that the game supervisor be involved in enforcing the rules.

The object:

The round is over when a player crosses the finish line. The next round begins with a new "traffic light."

Duck, Duck, Goose

Every player is engaged as a runner, a tagger or as a participant in joyful suspense and anticipation. This is a great introductory group game for young children. You can change the title to suit your own theme and it will still play well for a wide range of ages.

To start:

Have your group of 5-12 players sit in a wide circle. Designate one person to be the first "It" person. If your group is larger, create two or more circles with an "It" for each.

To play:

The "It" walks around the outside of the circle, gently tapping the others on the head and saying "Duck." At some point, the "It" taps someone and says "Goose." Goose stands up and chases "It" around the circle with the goal of tagging "It" before "It" reaches the vacant spot. If "It" sits down in the spot before Goose tags him/her, then Goose is "It." If Goose tags "It" before "It" sits down, then "It" remains "It" for another round.

The object:

Play until everyone has had a chance to be a tagger or until you get tired.

Acknowledgements

I must thank my Mother and Father for instilling in me a love for nature, the scientific method, physical activity and fun. My children and their friends have participated and contributed to my classes in many capacities for years. Isabella, Sophie, Sam and Emma: your help, presence, honest criticism and delight have shaped many of the activities in this book. I am grateful to Emma for coming down from Anchorage to do the marathon photoshoot that produced such beautiful pictures, and Yara and Gus for being so photogenic.

Shannon Buxton and Sue Hylen of the Bainbridge Island Metro Park and Recreation district have given me support and shared their knowledge and ideas to make so many of these activities possible. Thanks to Barbara Culler at the Children's Studies Program at Eastern Washington University who held my feet to the fire during the hard writing and gave me the chance to share my knowledge at Renton Technical College.

The students and families of Bainbridge Island, Seattle and the Puget Sound region have enjoyed, put up with, sat through, ran through and shaped my classes, camps and programs for years. I thank you. The pleasure has been all mine!

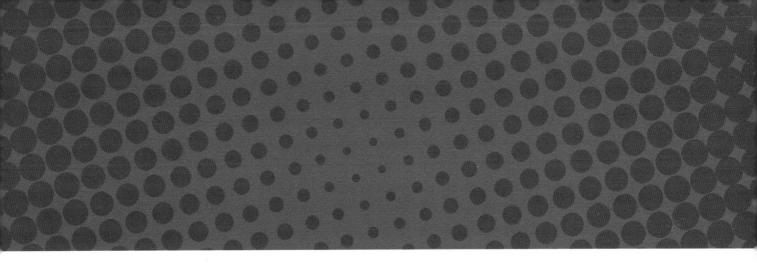

Photo credits:

Emma Agnes Sheffer – *many, many photos*

Sue Hylen – *parachute play*

Darlene Bose – *shaving cream*

Dallas Museum of Art – *vinegar play*

Stuart Anthony – *interstellar underdrive*

Beauty Playin' – *water canal*

Holger Zscheyge – *building blocks*

Jasper County Public Library – *marble run*

Banner Springs Library – *balloon rockets*

Peter Dutton – *Violet and the rocket balloon*

Li Tsin Soon – *savory pastry*

Timothy Lowell – *the rest*

About the Author

Tim Lowell has been leading art and science enrichment programs in Puget Sound schools since 2002. A teaching member of the Bainbridge Island Arts in Education consortium with a degree in Children's Studies from Eastern Washington University. Tim is a curriculum developer for the popular Curiosity Club elementary enrichment classes, Curiosity Camp Summer sessions and preschool science programs. He is a frequent speaker and workshop presenter at early childhood and elementary education conferences, sharing his lessons and ideas with other teachers. Tim believes that having fun with science, art and technology fosters lifelong appreciation and curiosity for learning.